Jewish
Slow Cooker
Recipes

Jewish Slow Cooker

Recipes

120 Holiday and Everyday Dishes Made Easy

LAURA FRANKEL

WILEY

John Wiley & Sons, Inc.

This book is printed on acid-free paper. ♾

Copyright © 2009 by Laura Frankel. All rights reserved.

Cover photos copyright © Ed Anderson.

Published by John Wiley & Sons, Inc., Hoboken, New Jersey.

Published simultaneously in Canada.

No part of this publication may be reproduced, stored in a retrieval system, or transmitted in any form or by any means, electronic, mechanical, photocopying, recording, scanning, or otherwise, except as permitted under Section 107 or 108 of the 1976 United States Copyright Act, without either the prior written permission of the Publisher, or authorization through payment of the appropriate per-copy fee to the Copyright Clearance Center, Inc., 222 Rosewood Drive, Danvers, MA 01923, (978) 750-8400, fax (978) 750-4470, or on the Web at www.copyright.com. Requests to the Publisher for permission should be addressed to the Permissions Department, John Wiley & Sons, Inc., 111 River Street, Hoboken, NJ 07030, (201) 748-6011, fax (201) 748-6008, or online at http://www.wiley.com/go/permissions.

Limit of Liability/Disclaimer of Warranty: While the publisher and author have used their best efforts in preparing this book, they make no representations or warranties with respect to the accuracy or completeness of the contents of this book and specifically disclaim any implied warranties of merchantability or fitness for a particular purpose. No warranty may be created or extended by sales representatives or written sales materials. The advice and strategies contained herein may not be suitable for your situation. You should consult with a professional where appropriate. Neither the publisher nor author shall be liable for any loss of profit or any other commercial damages, including but not limited to special, incidental, consequential, or other damages.

For general information on our other products and services or for technical support, please contact our Customer Care Department within the United States at (800) 762-2974, outside the United States at (317) 572-3993 or fax (317) 572-4002.

Wiley also publishes its books in a variety of electronic formats. Some content that appears in print may not be available in electronic books. For more information about Wiley products, visit our Web site at www.wiley.com.

Design: BTDNYC

Composition: Jeff Baker

Library of Congress Cataloging-in-Publication Data:

Frankel, Laura.
  Jewish slow cooker recipes / Laura Frankel.
      p. cm.
  Includes index.
  ISBN 978-0-470-26089-0 (cloth)
  1. Jewish cookery. 2. Kosher food. 3. Electric cookery, Slow. I. Title.
  TX724.F65 2009
  641.5'676—dc22

                                        2009004220

Printed in the United States of America

10 9 8 7 6 5 4 3 2 1

To

INA LOUISE MEYER

My earliest memories are of you creating amazing food

and of our families sharing wonderful meals.

You are missed by us all.

Contents

Acknowledgments

There are always many people behind the scenes making sure that everything is moving along smoothly, checking that everyone is on track and happy. This is true in kitchens as well as in life. The list of those who are near and dear to me and incredibly supportive is long. I could not dare to be as free with my ingredients or my words without all of you. You give me the courage to try and sometimes succeed and sometimes fail. Either way, it's all good. *L'Chaim!* To Life!

Zachary, Ari, and Jonah: Everything I do is with you three in mind. You are so completely awesome it often makes me speechless. Thank you for your support and patience.

Mom: Thank you for patiently dragging a stool to the kitchen counter to help me create another masterpiece when I was too young to reach. I am still trying to be like you, only I cook better.

Dennis Wasko: You really do put up with so much. You have been there through all of it. I simply could not do it without you and your support.

Kathy Wasko: Your undying encouragement gets me through the rough spots.

Dr. Donald and Julia Aaronson: You are like treasures and I am very lucky to call you friends. You are morally and spiritually uplifting and Julia, you are a fine hostess and chef. I am inspired daily by you both.

Wolfgang Puck: Chef, your demand for perfection has resulted in something very culturally and religiously special for the city of Chicago. Thank you.

Judith Weber: I appreciate your patient manner and encouraging comments. You see things in me that sometimes I cannot see. Thank you.

Karen Walanka: You have been there through thick and thin. You are true blue and so supportive. Thanks for always being there.

Dr. Reuven and Fay Weiss: Your friendship and support is truly appreciated and will never be forgotten.

Carlos Orjuela: I am often struck by your enthusiasm. You are always happy, even when we are in the weeds.

Matt Bencivenga: Chef, your creativity is inspirational. I love it!

Brent Anderson: Chef, you are the voice of calm in a stormy sea. Thanks for being there so many times.

Lucia Kelley: You always listen patiently while I give yet another impassioned speech about something or other.

Cheryl Desir: Oh, what fun we have each day! I raise my glass to your humor and sensibilities.

Kim and Alan Frankel: Thank you both for undying zeal and appetite for good kosher food for Chicago.

Ron and Cathy Silver: You guys are remarkable. I love your humor and wisdom. Cathy, I love our mornings at the farmers' market.

Norm and Leslie Finkel: Your support and enthusiasm are warm and comforting.

Edie and Murray Salzman: Your cholent parties are legendary and always hit the spot. They are as comfy as a fireplace and slippers. Love it!

Rabbi Sam Fraint: Your high expectations have set the bar and kept me moving along. I would not have done any of this without you.

Alan and Joan Sohn: Your constant support is like a great meal: very sustaining.

Stuart Dick: I love your clarity and timing. How do you always know when I need you?

Rabbi Yaakov Eisenbach: Rabbi, because of your support and wisdom, we have another kosher kitchen under our belts. *Yasher Koach!*

Marcia Seltzer Tobias: You have been a great friend, supporter, and part-time sous chef. Here's to many more happy times in kitchens in Chicago.

Avi Handelsman: Your kitchen is a great gathering place to learn, teach, and have fun.

Dr. Howard Sulkin: You never saw a reason why kosher food couldn't be as gourmet as any other food. Why doesn't everyone see that?

Sonia and Ted: I love how you let me exercise my creative side and are willing to just "go with it."

Rabbi Avi Finegold: You are one of the most inspirational foodies I have met in a long time. Keep on cooking and having fun in the kitchen.

All the foodies at Spertus Institute for Jewish Studies: I appreciate your support and interest in great-tasting and delicious kosher food.

Linda Ingroia: Thank you for your support, patience, and friendship. You always work with me and wait for me to get it right. Also at Wiley, Ava Wilder in production, Suzanne Sunwoo, Beth Tondreau, and Jeff Baker in design—thanks for pulling the book together beautifully.

Leah Koenig: I thought I was the only one who thought that kosher food had to be eco-conscious, all natural, organic, slow, local, sustainable, and delicious. Then I met you and read your amazing blog, The Jew & The Carrot. Thank you for keeping me on track with your thoughtful comments and your inspirational thinking.

Introduction

I *have been asked many times if I ever get tired of cooking. My response is always the same: No!* I know how lucky I am to do what I love and actually get paid for it. Cooking for me is like breathing. As a professional chef, I cook all day long and often into the night, but I don't mind the long hours. I get into my groove and just keep going, getting a thrill out of watching individual components of a meal come together to create a feast.

When I opened my first restaurant in 1999, I was driven not only by my love of cooking, but by the desire to prove that kosher food can be as gourmet and exciting as any other type of modern and "edgy" food. I still am. I want to provide the best kosher food possible for my customers, using only the freshest and highest-quality ingredients. The same goes in my household. When my family decided to keep kosher, we agreed to give up eating pork, shellfish, and the combination of meat and dairy. We did not give up flavor.

While I know that I am fortunate to have the job I do, sometimes those long hours can take a toll on meal preparation at home. I simply don't have the time to stand in my kitchen and prepare the delicious, wholesome, and—dare I say?—adventurous food I love. From time to time, I still do spend long hours in my home kitchen. And other times a simple salad and sandwich does the trick, though I try to stay away from convenience foods that are loaded with salt, fat, and additives. (I always feel shortchanged after warming up a flavorless frozen dinner.) But there have been many moments when I simply felt like I did not have time to deliver the meal that my family and friends deserved.

Then one day, the answer struck me—the slow cooker. The very same piece of equipment I have used every Shabbat for years. As a Sabbath-observant Jew and mother, I cannot imagine what our Shabbat lunches would be like without our slow cooker. There is real comfort in knowing that, despite not being able to cook on Shabbat, a warm and comforting lunch awaits us on Saturday afternoon. The trick was realizing I could use this Shabbat miracle machine every day of the week.

The slow cooker essentially acts like another pair of hands—a friend stirring the pot while you attend to other things. Unlike their predecessors from the 1950s, today's slow cookers are high tech. My mother's slow cooker tended to produce gummy meat and vegetable stews that kept me from taking slow cooking seriously for many years. My slow cooker has timers, thermostats, and a variety of temperature settings that help meat and hearty root vegetables maintain their textures as well as their flavor. Thank goodness for technology.

The slow cooker food of the past was not the slow cooker's fault. Let's just chalk it up to an era when kitchen technique, ingredi-ents, and culinary courage were less developed. Today's slow cooker food is bold, assertive, and more enticing. My slow cooker has assisted in many of my favorite dishes such as Lamb Tagine (page 104), succulent Garlicky Pot Roast (page 68), and a slew of nuanced, flavorful soups.

Most of the recipes in this book are written to be prepared in a slow cooker. Some of the recipes may seem a bit complicated at first, but once you break them down into steps, they are actually quite simple. I have also included some recipes that are not prepared in a slow cooker but pair well with slow-cooked meals. Every entrée, soup, and dessert in the book can prepared without the addition of these complementary recipes, but in my opinion, they often "make the dish." Duck Confit (page 122) is a dynamite treat unto itself, but with the addition of some Moroccan spices and Sweet-Tart Orange Sauce (page 120), the dish becomes fiercely flavorful. Similarly, slathering my Creamy Coleslaw (page 149) on a bun and pairing it with Rubbed Brisket (page 64) turns the succulent meat into the quintessential crunchy sandwich. By planning a little and making double batches of some items, weekday meals never need to be boring or short-changed.

The recipes in this book are accessible to eaters of all backgrounds; all recipes also follow the kosher guidelines that are important to me and my family. While this book is not meant to be a kosher primer, it is important to state some of the basics:

- The laws of kashrut come primarily from the book of Leviticus in the Bible, which lists the animals considered kosher and those that are not. In order for an animal to be kosher, it must have split hooves and chew its cud.
- There are three categories of food in kashrut: meat, dairy, and pareve. Pareve refers to foods that are "neutral" (containing neither dairy nor meat) and can be eaten with any meal. Eggs, fish, grains, fruits, and vegetables are pareve, although it is not acceptable to eat fish and meat off the same plate. A passage in Deuteronomy states that you may not cook a kid in its mother's milk, so it is forbidden to eat milk and meat at the same time or to cook them in the same meal.
- The way an animal is raised does not influence its kosher status, but an animal must be slaughtered in a ritual manner by a *shochet* (a specially trained observant individual who performs the slaughter). The "life" blood must be drained from the animal and the meat must be salted to remove any traces of blood.
- Poultry—mainly chicken and duck—follows similar laws. Domesticated fowl are kosher when slaughtered and salted in the same manner as meat.
- Kosher-observant Jews can only eat eggs and milk that came from a kosher animal.
- Fish with scales and fins are permitted. Some fish have scales that they shed at a later stage of development; those fish are prohibited. Shellfish are never kosher. While meat and poultry must usually be purchased from a kosher butcher or supermarket with a kosher section, fish can be purchased from any fishmonger or grocery store.

For an in-depth description of the kosher laws, I suggest *How to Keep Kosher* by Lisë Stern. There are also many online sources, and a rabbi can offer direction and guidance.

Slow Cooker Basics

I'll admit: I sometimes feel like a kitchen floozy. I simply fall in love with new cooking tools too easily, eagerly awaiting the arrival of kitchen catalogues with their glossy photos and intriguing descriptions. I stalk the high-tech gadget stores like a hunter after his prey. Who could blame me for wanting the newest and latest kitchen gear? But these relationships are often fleeting. My once-adored waffle machine becomes a dust collector; my fancy coffee pot with all the bells and whistles is cast aside for a simple French press pot.

After all, my counter space is precious and I am simply too busy to bother. These short-lived love affairs have been repeated many times and with many gadgets—except for one: my love for the honest, hardworking slow cooker remains true blue.

As an equipment junkie, I have always owned a slow cooker. To be fair, I have to say I also own just about every piece of kitchen equipment ever created. But kitchen equipment fads change just as often as fashion. I have often joked about my mother "wokking" chicken every day for a year. But my slow cooker has remained my steady sidekick, and just as my sharpest knives will never get too much rest, so too will the slow cooker with a permanent spot on my countertop.

A slow cooker is a thermostatically controlled electric countertop appliance that consists of three parts:

- a lid made of metal, glass, or plastic
- an insert made of glazed ceramic, metal, or plastic
- a housing unit fitted with a heating element

Slow cookers come in a variety of sizes ranging from a three-cup unit to one that holds up to seven quarts, and in two shapes, round or oval.

Slow cookers cook at two temperatures: Low and High. Some have warming tempera-

tures that are perfect for buffet use and holding food at a safe temperature for mealtime.

Because heat takes a long time to build up in the slow cooker and the steam that forms not only aids in the cooking process but also allows a vacuum to form under the lid, I do not recommend lifting the lid to check on the cooking process. Every time the lid is lifted, you'll need an additional twenty minutes for the slow cooker to come back to the ideal cooking temperature.

But don't worry: Slow cooking is similar to braising in an oven. You just need to assemble the ingredients as the recipe states and the cooker will do all the work perfectly.

I consider the slow cooker as a possible sous chef any time there is a cooking period of more than an hour. I am a professional chef, a mother, a part-time carpooler, and a constant schlepper. I frequently don't have time to watch pots, and even when I do, I really prefer to relax with my kids. I love the fact that I can take a tough cut of meat and have it fork-tender without fussing over it or even watching it.

While writing this book, I tried every slow cooker on the market—frequently several of them simultaneously. I got great results from every cooker, including Calphalon, but one stood out as my favorite. All-Clad makes a 6½-quart oval model that is similar to other brands, but with a twist. The insert is made of Teflon-coated aluminum. The thrill of this innovation is that the insert can be used on a burner to brown meat and vegetables and then placed into the housing unit. This is truly one-pot cookery. I am not afraid of hard kitchen work or dish washing, but I have to admit I am smitten by convenience. It is pretty irresistible to have a piece of equipment that is time saving and efficient. While the All-Clad slow cooker is a bit expensive, I find that the ease of the insert doubling as a sauté pan balances out the price.

Many of the recipes in this book require a large slow cooker, the 6½-quart model, while others are perfectly suited to smaller cookers. The recipes that mention a specific size slow cooker have large yields or use larger cuts of meat or poultry that require more room. I wrote the recipes for yields of four or more servings. Many of these recipes can be cut in half and cooked in a smaller slow cooker. Just as with any new piece of kitchen equipment, it may take some experimenting to get the amount of liquid just right. The surface area of each cooker varies slightly. If you find you have too much liquid at the end of a recipe, simply transfer the liquid to a saucepan and reduce it over medium-high heat. It is hard to have too little liquid with slow cooker cooking. The machine does not allow for evaporation. But if a dish seems a bit dry, just add a bit of chicken stock or water.

I have my cooking process down to a science: I heat up the insert, lightly coat the bottom with oil, and brown my meat. I always have a sheet pan or bowl nearby to hold each batch of browned food. At the end of the browning, I drain off any excess fat and place all of the ingredients back into the cooker.

Though slow cookers work wonders with meat, I recommend trying the slow cooker for dairy dishes, too. Slow-cooked Wild Mushroom Stroganoff (page 130) is delicious and hearty. My family craves Maple-Pecan Bread Pudding (page 176) with leftover challah made gooey, fragrant, and comforting with butter, cream, and a luxurious cooking session in the slow cooker.

I also recommend a slow cooker for holidays, particularly Passover. I look forward to Passover. Not only do I enjoy the holiday and the time with my family; I love the ability to plug in my slow cooker and let it do all the work while I enjoy my time off from my day job. Passover slow cooker food is not boring or plain. Not when I'm cooking, and it doesn't have to be for you either. Artichoke Caponata (page 16) is exciting and fresh as a spring day—and really easy with the slow cooker. That's just one new idea for Passover.

If you're a slow cooker fan, I am sure you will find new exciting recipes in this book. If you are a bit more cautious, then maybe you will find the inspiration to try slow cooking with the words of one of my recipe testers when she said, "I never knew gadget cookery could be so heavenly and gourmet!" She was new to the slow cooker and now owns several.

BROWNING = FLAVOR

Of all the techniques for cooking meat and vegetables, nothing is more important than browning. This is especially true of food to be cooked in the slow cooker. Deep, luxurious flavor is something that I associate with slow-cooked food—but only if some preliminary steps are taken. Every cook has experienced the sensation of simple pieces of meat or vegetables turning mouthwateringly tempting when the surface becomes crusty and brown in a hot pan or over a grill. (Contrary to popular belief, the crust does not seal in the juices. It does, however, caramelize the sugars and oxidize the proteins in the meat, resulting in a very aromatic and tasty final dish.)

The perfect cuts of meat for slow cooking and braising tend to be cheaper, tougher, and full of hidden flavor. Braising employs two types of heat:

first a dry heat while the meat is browned, and then a moist heat when the meat is covered with a flavorful liquid. The long, slow "dunk" in liquid helps draw the collagens out of the meat, which results in a luxurious, satisfying sauce. The deepened flavor comes from the crucial step of browning. Browning the meat before putting it into the slow cooker helps to coax out its fullest flavor even before it starts to soften.

To brown meat properly, start with a room-temperature piece of meat—it is more relaxed and flexible, and the natural juices are evenly distributed.

Choose a pan that is large enough to allow for space around and in between the pieces of food you are browning. (When using a separate sauté pan, avoid nonstick types as the surface will prevent the meat from forming a crust.) If you are browning separate pieces of meat rather than one large roast, you will need to do the browning in batches. Too much food in the pan lowers the heat and could end up steaming it.

Place the pan over medium-high heat and once it is hot, add enough oil to lightly coat the bottom of the pan. (A cold pan will cause the meat to stick and tear when you try to turn it.) Pat the meat dry, even if it has been marinated, since moisture will create steam and can cause the meat to stick to the pan. Season the meat with salt, freshly ground pepper, and any other seasonings you are using.

Gently place the meat into the pan. Browning happens fairly quickly, so pay attention to avoid burning the meat. After several minutes, gently raise the end of the meat and check to see if it has browned. If so, then turn it to continue browning on all sides. I recommend checking beef after about five minutes per side, and three minutes for poultry.

Once the meat has browned, remove it from the pan. The browned bits in the bottom of the pan are caramelized pieces of meat and are loaded with flavor. They are traditionally called *sucs* (pronounced *sooks*), from the word *sucre* (sugar) in French. To gather the browned bits, you can add wine, stock, or water in a pinch. Cook over medium heat, lightly scraping up the browned bits with a wooden spatula or spoon. Most of these tasty little morsels of protein dissolve during the deglazing process, producing a very aromatic *fond* (foundation) for sauces. Just add the deglazed browned bits and liquid to your slow cooker.

The same browning techniques used for meat may also be used for most fish, vegetables, and fruit. Most fishes are delicate and will require much less time to brown.

Stocking Your Pantry

I once taught a cooking class for a group at someone's home. Before the class, I sent the hostess a list of ingredients that I would need, and she took care of the shopping. The night of the class, when I asked for the chicken stock (I was praying for homemade), I was appalled that she pulled out bouillon cubes and a pot of hot water. But I regained my composure and told her that she was lucky I had arrived in time. I quickly cut up the chickens I was going to use in the demo, added some vegetables, and had a more satisfying batch of stock going in no time. I am not against saving time in the kitchen, but chicken stock comes from chickens, not from pressed cubes of salt, fat, and chemicals. The experience reminded me that it's worth repeating that a well-stocked pantry is essential to any home cook and especially to the home cook who is short on time.

Here are the basic components of a well-stocked pantry.

CANNED TOMATO PRODUCTS

While I almost always prefer fresh fruits and vegetables to frozen or canned, I love many quality canned tomato products. One exception is tomato sauce, which tends to have too much salt in it and someone else's preferred flavor profile. However, I think that a pantry is not complete without a great tomato paste and whole peeled plum tomatoes. They help give many sauces a rich mouthfeel and deliver a small amount of concentrated sweetness.

For better flavor and texture, use whole peeled tomatoes rather than crushed tomatoes. I drain the tomatoes, transfer them to a bowl, and squeeze them with clean hands to crush them into smaller pieces. Others use kitchen scissors to cut the tomatoes. You can choose. Either way, they don't end up too mushy, the way canned crushed tomatoes can be.

If you want an instant reminder of summer, try adding sun-dried tomatoes to a dish. Sun-dried tomatoes are sweet and tangy with a chewy, raisiny texture. I add them to soups and chicken, veal, and fish dishes. They are also delicious cut up and sprinkled on salads.

Sun-dried tomatoes are available packed in either olive or sunflower oil. They are also packaged dry. To use the oil-packed variety, drain the oil from the tomatoes and be sure to reserve the oil for use in salad dressings or for sautéing. If you use the dry variety, first add the tomatoes to a small amount of simmering water and allow them to steep for 15 minutes to soften.

CHOCOLATE

A good pantry should also include some dessert goodies. High-quality chocolate is a must—there is simply no excuse to use the cheap waxy kind—and luckily there are plenty of great kosher chocolates on the market. I prefer the Belgian Callebaut, which I have used for more than ten years. I use it in my professional kitchens and at home. I prefer the bittersweet chocolate with a high cocoa content of 60 to 70 percent.

One of my favorite pantry staples is deep, rich cocoa powder. I always use Valrhona cocoa powder. It has an intense, almost tropical smell and flavor. I have tried many cocoa powders and this is the one that I always come back to.

DRIED MUSHROOMS

Dried mushrooms are like treasure to me. I am an avid user of porcini mushrooms in my slow cooker. Their intense woodsy flavor pairs well with everything. The long slow-cooking process allows the porcinis to perfume meats and sauces without overwhelming them.

My second favorite dried mushrooms are dried chanterelles. These mushrooms are buttery-apricoty in flavor and fragrance. They are more delicate than porcinis but equally wonderful.

Dried mushrooms are expensive, but they are worth it; a little goes a long way—just a few crumbled pieces add lots of flavor. I try to stock up on dried mushrooms when they are on sale and also purchase them in pieces, which tend to be less expensive than whole. Mushroom pieces do not have the visual appeal of the whole mushroom, but who cares? They are meant to flavor my dinner with a rich, earthy essence, not be the visual star of it.

GOOD-QUALITY GRAINS

Every pantry should also have grains, pastas, beans, and a variety of rice. I like the idea of being able to pull out some brown rice and turn it into a master side dish with the simple addition of a few spices. While the kosher laws dictate many of the ingredients an observant Jew can use, grains and starches level the playing field.

SALT

Kosher salt is not just for kosher kitchens. As a professional chef, I have spent a lot of time in kitchens around the world and found that most chefs "worth their salt" cook with kosher salt. I recommend keeping a small dish of kosher salt near your stovetop so that while you are sautéing or making sauces you can season as you go. Sea salt is great for garnishing—I love sprinkling the crunchy crystals on top of prepared meals. While cooking, however, kosher salt is the way to go.

SPICES

Almost every recipe in this book calls for spices, herbs, or a combination of both. In my first book, *Jewish Cooking for All Seasons*, I wrote, "Spice is the variety of life," and I still believe that. Spices and herbs give a dish personality and character and can evoke memories of great vacations, meals, and family events. A well-stocked pantry should include the best versions of basic herbs and spices. For example, I think many cooks have been misled to believe that store-bought ground pepper is just fine in a dish. However, whole peppercorns are tiny, flavor-packed dried berries that add a totally different pungent warm fruitiness to any dish. When they are freshly cracked or ground, they deliver more flavor and complex aroma to food than any preground product. (See Sources, page 233.)

VANILLA

High-quality vanilla extract and vanilla beans are vital to any kitchen. The good stuff costs a bit more because it is simply a better product. Vanilla is derived from an orchid plant. The extract should smell exotically floral. This luscious aroma and flavor result in equally amazing baked products. Remember, any ingredient you put into a recipe should be at its peak of ripeness and the best you can afford. Slow-cooked baked goods have a very pronounced vanilla flavor. The small amount of alcohol in the vanilla does not burn off as quickly and the essence of vanilla seems to be more distinct. My favorite vanilla extract is from Nielsen-Massey. The extract comes from different vanilla beans from around the world and each one has its own character and perfume. (See Sources, page 233.)

WINE

Good wine is one of the fundamental building blocks of a great sauce. You simply cannot start a sauce with poor-quality or even so-so wine. Good wine comes from good grapes. I recommend purchasing wine from a winery that grows its grapes. A winemaker who is fretting over his or her grapes is going to make great wine. Kosher wines have gone from just okay to really amazing in the last decade.

For cooking in the slow cooker I recommend a wine that is fairly dry and has a high alcohol content. A very sugary wine or one with a low alcohol content is not going to make a good sauce for beef or poultry. A drier wine will be a bit more complex with some nuance of flavor and fragrance. That being said, you don't need to spend a fortune on wine for cooking. I like to use moderately priced table wines—the same assertive wines that I would drink with dinner. Slow-cooked meats have a lot of flavor, especially when they are cooked with garlic, onions, and herbs. When buying wine for your pantry, make sure you purchase bottles that can stand up to all of that flavor. I am a fan of red zinfandel and cabernet sauvignon from California. I also like a merlot from Israel that has a complex flavor. For white wines I recommend California chardonnay. The toasty, buttery flavor pairs well with chicken, veal, and fish.

Absent from this list are what I call "faux" foods. I do not cook with margarine, fake dairy products, or other common substitute ingredients. There is a widespread notion that if a recipe calls for butter, then margarine is the perfect stand-in, and likewise cream and nondairy whipped topping. I have said it before and I will say it again: Butter is simply the best for baking, and there is no substitute for cream. What you can do instead is to search for recipes that utilize other ingredients. When I bake pareve desserts I look for recipes that use oils for fats, chiffon-style cakes, and fruit-based desserts. I use butter when a recipe calls for it and I enjoy it—a lot! When I eat meat, I don't bake dairy desserts and try to pretend that they are great with substitute laboratory ingredients. I urge everyone who keeps kosher to feed their families and friends only the most delicious and natural foods available. Keep your food real. It will

not only taste better and you will never have to say that it "is great, for pareve," but it will be healthier, too.

Seasonal Key

"Seasonal ingredients" refers to vegetables and fruits that are harvested at their peak and to seafood and meats that are available only at certain times of year, when they are most abundant and at their best. Seasonal eating has been practiced since ancient times, when people ate what the earth provided at one time of year or another. Food eaten at its peak tastes better, is more nutritious, and is cheaper. Eating seasonally can be very exciting as you learn to take advantage of ingredients during their peak and experiment with new ingredients.

Recipes that include seasonal ingredients will be marked with one or more of these symbols:

 Spring

 Summer

 Fall

 Winter

Recipes that can be made all year long will show all four seasons.

Appetizers

Anyone can cook—only the fearless can be great.
—CHEF AUGUSTE GUSTEAU, *RATATOUILLE*

The slow cooker has been a lifesaver on so many occasions. Keeping my guests happy while I finish dinner is no exception; I do that with tempting appetizers. For example, I love homemade hummos, but hate the flavor of canned chick peas. I also don't enjoy taking up an entire burner for hours while dried chick peas turn from impenetrable balls to creamy nuggets of nutty goodness. I can, however, enjoy the same results in the slow cooker.

I have included some simple dips and garnishes that are not made in the slow cooker. I added these recipes as I feel that they "gild" the lily perfectly. The slow cooker recipes that they are meant to go with are delicious and wonderful on their own. But if you make certain dishes over and over (because they are beloved), it's nice to enhance them in different ways. You can add one of these recipes to make a rewarding difference.

HUMMOS

PAREVE

MAKES 2 ¹/₂ CUPS

Homemade hummos with freshly cooked chick peas is a staple in our home and in my professional kitchen. I will admit to occasionally taking a kitchen shortcut here and there, but using canned chick peas is never an option. There really is no comparison in flavor or texture between the freshly cooked and canned varieties. With a little planning and the use of the slow cooker, it is easy to prepare usually long-cooking chick peas and this delicious dip.

**1 pound dried chick peas, sorted through
    and soaked overnight**

⅓ cup tahini

2 garlic cloves, chopped

¼ cup fresh lemon juice

**¼ cup extra-virgin olive oil, plus addition-
    al for garnish**

**1 tablespoon toasted cumin seeds (see
    page 199), ground**

**Kosher salt and freshly ground black
    pepper**

Za'atar (page 203)

SUGGESTED ACCOMPANIMENTS

Toasted pita crisps, flatbreads,
vegetable crudités

① Preheat the slow cooker to Low.

② Drain the chick peas and transfer them to the slow cooker insert. Add 6 cups of water, cover, and cook on Low for 6 hours, until the chick peas are tender and not grainy when squeezed between your fingers.

③ Drain the chick peas. Place the chick peas, tahini, garlic, lemon juice, ¼ cup oil, and cumin in a food processor. Process until the mixture is very creamy. (You may have to do this in batches or place the ingredients in a large bowl and use an immersion blender.) Adjust the seasoning with salt and pepper. Transfer the hummos to a storage container. To keep it from drying out, press parchment paper or plastic wrap onto the surface of the hummos, then seal the container. Store in the refrigerator for up to 5 days.

④ To serve the hummos, mound it on a platter or in a bowl. Drizzle the surface with extra-virgin olive oil and sprinkle generously with za'atar. Serve with your choice of accompaniments.

CHEESE FONDUE

This versatile recipe is a quick go-to dish for a lazy Sunday afternoon game day, or as an elegant appetizer. The slow cooker is the perfect tool for melting cheese at exactly the right temperature and rate. "Slow and easy" ensures that the cheese will be creamy and smooth.

My version of the classic Swiss dish is zesty and sharp with the addition of beer and hot sauce. The beer may be replaced with apple juice if desired.

1 garlic clove, cut in half

¾ cup dark beer such as Guinness or Aventinus, or apple juice

2 cups shredded Swiss cheese (½ pound)

1 cup shredded sharp white Cheddar cheese (¼ pound)

¼ cup grated Parmesan cheese, preferably Parmigiano-Reggiano

1 tablespoon cornstarch

2 teaspoons Harissa (page 181) or hot sauce

Freshly ground black pepper

DAIRY

SUGGESTED ACCOMPANIMENTS
Cubes of hearty bread, toasted pita, bagel chips, cooked new potatoes, crunchy vegetable crudités, cut-up apples and pears

1. Rub the inside of a small slow cooker insert with the garlic. Discard the garlic.
2. Pour the beer into the slow cooker insert.
3. In a large bowl, toss the cheeses with the cornstarch, taking care to coat all of the cheese with the cornstarch. Add the cheeses to the beer in the slow cooker. Cover and cook on Low for 1 hour.
4. Stir the cheese; add the harissa and black pepper to taste. Cover and cook for 15 minutes more.
5. To serve the fondue, remove the cover and keep the slow cooker on Low. Serve with your choice of accompaniments.

ARTICHOKE CAPONATA

PAREVE

MAKES ABOUT 4 CUPS

This is essentially a relish of vegetables. While most caponatas feature tomatoes and eggplant, they can really include anything in season. This brightly flavored version is a concoction of late winter and early spring vegetables, delicious as a first-course salad or topper for your favorite flatbreads or crostini. I serve it with roasted chicken, duck, and even fish. It adds springtime flair to any table, and for Passover we drizzle our matzah with olive oil and herbs and then dollop some of this caponata on top for a crunchy snack.

The caponata can be stored in the refrigerator, covered, for up to 3 days.

Olive oil

1 medium fennel bulb, trimmed, cored, and sliced into thin strips (reserve the fronds for garnish)

2 medium leeks, white part only, chopped

3 garlic cloves, finely chopped

1 tablespoon tomato paste

½ cup dry white wine such as chardonnay

½ cup golden raisins

1 pound (12 to 14) baby artichokes or frozen artichoke hearts, thawed

Juice of 1 lemon

¼ cup toasted pine nuts (see page 199)

¼ cup fresh mint leaves, torn or cut into thin strips

½ cup chopped fresh flat-leaf parsley

2 tablespoons chopped fresh thyme

Kosher salt and freshly ground black pepper

SUGGESTED GARNISHES

Olive oil, reserved chopped fennel fronds, chopped mint

1. Preheat a slow cooker to High.
2. Place a large sauté pan over medium-high heat. Lightly coat the bottom of the pan with olive oil. Cook the fennel and leeks until lightly browned and softened, about 5 minutes. Stir in the garlic, tomato paste, wine, and raisins and continue cooking for 1 minute more.
3. Transfer the mixture to the slow cooker insert. Cover and cook on High for 3 hours.

4 To clean the fresh artichokes, use a paring knife to cut the outside leaves free from the body of the vegetable. Continue turning your knife around the artichoke until you have an equal amount of green leaves with yellow tops. Leave the stem intact—it gives the artichoke a pretty shape. If you like, peel some of the tough green fibers from the outside of the stem with a paring knife. Cut the artichoke in half lengthwise and scoop out the choke (if any) with a melon baller. Place the artichoke pieces in a bowl of cold water with the lemon juice to keep the artichokes from turning dark.

5 Add the pine nuts, artichokes, mint, parsley, and thyme to the vegetable mixture. Add salt and pepper to taste. Cover and cook on High for 1 hour more.

6 Serve the caponata warm or cold. Drizzle with additional olive oil, and garnish with fennel fronds or chopped mint, if desired.

MIXED OLIVE TAPENADE

PAREVE

MAKES ³/₄ CUP

This is one of my favorite simple dishes. I like to keep it around to smear on crostini, to top fish dishes like Olive Oil–Poached Halibut (page 125), or to garnish White Bean Ragù (see page 101). Because the tapenade is made mostly from pantry ingredients, you can have it at your fingertips anytime.

This tapenade can be stored in the refrigerator, covered, for up to 3 weeks.

½ cup pitted kalamata olives

½ cup pitted cracked green olives

Juice and coarsely chopped zest of
    1 lemon

1 whole peeled garlic clove

2 oil-packed anchovy fillets, drained,
    rinsed, dried, and chopped

Extra-virgin olive oil

2 tablespoons finely chopped shallot
    (1 small shallot)

¼ cup chopped fresh flat-leaf parsley

Kosher salt and freshly ground black
    pepper

½ teaspoon chili flakes (optional)

1. Place the olives, lemon juice and zest, garlic, and anchovies in a food processor. Pulse the mixture until it resembles a chunky paste. Add olive oil if necessary.

2. Transfer the mixture to a small bowl. Stir in the shallot and parsley. Adjust the seasoning with salt and pepper. Stir in the chili flakes, if using. Transfer the tapenade to a storage container. To keep it from drying out, press parchment paper or plastic wrap onto the surface of the tapenade, then seal the container.

SUN-DRIED TOMATO TAPENADE

MAKES ¹/₄ CUP

PAREVE

My love for all things tomato is no secret—I simply cannot get enough of that flavor. Sun-dried tomatoes are no exception to my arsenal of tomato products. I prefer to use the type stored in fruity olive oil, which packs the tapenade with extra flavor. This particular recipe is delicious with fish or chicken. I like to serve it with Olive Oil–Poached Halibut (page 125) or on top of Smoky Navy Beans with Eggplant Ragù (page 132).

This tapenade can be stored in the refrigerator, covered, for up to 2 weeks.

½ cup sun-dried tomatoes in olive oil,
    drained (oil reserved)
1 garlic clove, chopped
1 tablespoon tomato paste
3 tablespoons chopped fresh flat-leaf
    parsley
1 tablespoon capers, drained and rinsed
Kosher salt and freshly ground black
    pepper

① Place the sun-dried tomatoes, garlic, and tomato paste in a food processor. Pulse until the mixture comes together and forms a paste. Add a small amount of the reserved oil to achieve the right consistency.

② Stir in the parsley and capers. Season to taste with salt and pepper. Transfer the tapenade to a storage container. To keep it from drying out, press parchment paper or plastic wrap onto the surface of the tapenade, then seal the container.

CHEF LAURA'S
FAMOUS GUACAMOLE

PAREVE

MAKES 2 CUPS

The secret to good guacamole is simple: the ingredients should be ripe and really fresh, and each bite or scoopful should burst with flavor. This means no powdered garlic allowed and lots of tasting, to make sure the flavors are well balanced. My kids eat guacamole as a healthy snack, and sometimes use it instead of mustard or mayonnaise for really delicious meat or dairy sandwiches. The best time of year to find good avocados is in the summer. Scoop them up while you can because the pickings are slim and expensive in the winter. I have included this delicious recipe in this book, though it is not made in a slow cooker, as I could not imagine a festive Mexican meal without this creamy dip.

Contrary to popular food myth, leaving the pit in the bowl of guacamole will not prevent the avocados from oxidizing and turning black. To ensure that your guacamole stays green, cover the guacamole with plastic wrap or parchment paper and lightly press the wrap directly on the surface. Then go ahead and throw out the pit, or plant it.

3 ripe avocados, peeled and pitted
¼ cup fresh lime juice

2 tablespoons best-quality extra-virgin olive oil
2 garlic cloves, creamed (see page 21)
2 medium tomatillos, husks removed, cut into small dice
6 cherry tomatoes, quartered
1 small red onion, finely diced
½ jalapeño pepper, seeded and diced very small
¼ cup chopped fresh cilantro
2 radishes, diced very small (optional)
Kosher salt and freshly ground black pepper

SUGGESTED ACCOMPANIMENTS
Crispy tortilla chips, jícama strips, cucumber slices, radishes, carrot strips

1. Place the avocados into a large bowl. Add the lime juice, olive oil, and garlic.
2. Mash the mixture with a potato masher or fork until it is mostly mashed but some chunks remain. Add the tomatillos, tomatoes, onion, jalapeño, cilantro, and radishes, if using. Stir them in to combine. Adjust the seasoning with salt and pepper. Serve with your choice of accompaniments.

GUACAMOLE ESSENTIALS
Avocados

How do you find a ripe avocado? Give it a squeeze. Ripe avocados will yield slightly under gentle pressure, but maintain a somewhat firm consistency. You can also pull out the stem piece and check to see if it is green underneath. If it is green the avocado will be ripe, but if it is black the avocado is past its prime.

Creamed Garlic

Avoid chunks of garlic in your guacamole by trying this great knife trick: Coarsely chop the garlic. Add a little kosher salt to the pile of garlic and continue chopping and rubbing the flat part of your knife against the chunks. The salt acts as an abrasive and after several minutes the garlic will turn into a creamy puree that will disappear into your guacamole, leaving behind a powerful garlic punch.

PARMESAN CRISPS

MAKES 8 CRISPS

These salty, nutty crisps can be baked several days ahead of serving and kept at room temperature in an airtight container. While the crisps are not made in the slow cooker, they are great with Artichoke Caponata (page 16), many tapenadas and dips, and they nicely embellish the Italian Pumpkin Soup (page 52) with their earthy crunch and lacy texture.

**3 ounces Parmesan cheese, preferably
Parmigiano-Reggiano, grated
(about 1 cup)**

**1 tablespoon freshly ground black
pepper**

1. Preheat the oven to 300°F.
2. Line a baking sheet with two sheets of parchment paper. Place 2 tablespoons of grated cheese in mounds on the baking sheet. You should have 8 mounds.
3. Flatten each mound with the back of a spoon and sprinkle with the pepper.
4. Bake for 5 to 6 minutes, until lightly golden. Allow to cool before handling.

ROSEMARY AND PARMESAN POPCORN

DAIRY

MAKES 3 ¾ CUPS

This recipe began as a fun garnish for my Creamy Tomato Soup (page 39) for my kids. I think it was one of those nights where we all needed something different and I hadn't planned anything special. So I popped some corn, tossed it quickly with rosemary and Parmesan cheese, and everyone was happy. Now, it's a frequent snack request.

Canola oil
¼ cup unpopped popcorn, preferably an organic heirloom variety
1 tablespoon chopped fresh rosemary
2 tablespoons grated Parmesan cheese, preferably Parmigiano-Reggiano
1 tablespoon unsalted butter, melted
Lots of freshly cracked black peppercorns

1. Place a medium saucepan over medium heat. Lightly coat the bottom of the pan with canola oil. Add the popcorn and cover the pan so that a crack remains open. This allows the steam to escape and keeps the popcorn from getting tough.

2. Shake the pan periodically until the corn starts to pop. Continue shaking the pan until the corn popping slows down. Remove from the heat and allow the corn to finish popping.

3. Transfer the popped corn to a large bowl and sprinkle with the rosemary, Parmesan cheese, and melted butter. Finish with cracked pepper. Toss lightly. Serve with Creamy Tomato Soup or any other dairy dish where you need something whimsical.

HOT WINGS

Hot wings are a tasty, roll-up-your-sleeves kind of dish. Once you start eating my addictive spicy and sweet version, you might not be able to stop. They are a treat for game day or any-time you need good party grub.

24 chicken wing drums (see Note)

3 tablespoons All-Purpose Spice Rub (page 197)

2 tablespoons Harissa (page 181)

2 tablespoons rice vinegar

1 tablespoon neutral-flavored oil such as canola

3 tablespoons honey

Kosher salt and freshly ground black pepper

Herbed Aïoli Dipping Sauce (page 186; optional)

1 Preheat the broiler to High. Preheat the slow cooker to High.

2 Rinse and pat the chicken wings thoroughly dry with paper towels. Generously rub the all-purpose rub on the wings and set aside.

MEAT

3 Place a small saucepan over medium heat and add the harissa, vinegar, oil, and honey. Whisk together and add salt and pepper to taste. Heat just until combined. Remove from the heat and set aside.

4 Line a sheet pan with aluminum foil. Space the wings out on the pan. Place under the broiler and broil for 3 minutes per side until browned and crisp.

5 Toss the wings with half of the sauce in the slow cooker insert. Cover and cook on Low for 4 to 5 hours or on High for 2 hours.

6 Serve with the remaining sauce as a dipping sauce and with Herbed Aïoli Dipping Sauce, if you like.

NOTE

▶ Chicken wings actually come in three sections; the tip, the flat, and the drum, though I very rarely see a kosher wing with the tip on it. The flats and drums can be purchased separately or still joined together. I use both, but prefer the drums for this recipe: The drums resemble a drumstick with a little handle that keeps your fingers from getting too messy. The flats are the middle joint between the tip and the drums and while tasty, they don't have much meat on them. The drums have more meat on them. I generally save the flats in a bag in the freezer for chicken stock.

VIP KREPLACH WITH SHORT RIBS

MAKES ABOUT 75 KREPLACH

Once I found out how easy it was to make these tasty little dumpling treasures, I started stocking them in my freezer. No longer reserved for High Holiday soup garnishes, we eat them as snacks and appetizers. By preparing the meat in my slow cooker, half the work is done for me. I usually make my own kreplach dough, but also have been known to use wonton skins in a pinch. I make a big batch of the meat and freeze it in small portions. That way I always have richly flavored meat to concoct homemade dumplings in a snap.

For a crispy side dish or appetizer, after boiling them, finish the kreplach in batches over medium heat in a sauté pan lightly coated with olive oil until lightly browned and slightly crisped on both sides.

You'll need to prepare the dough at least one day ahead to give it a chance to rest.

Olive oil

3 pounds short ribs

3 medium Spanish onions, thinly sliced

6 garlic cloves, grated with a Microplane

½ cup Essential Chicken Stock (page 207)

Kosher salt and freshly ground black pepper

Kreplach Dough (recipe follows) or 1 package wonton skins

Warm water, for sealing the kreplach

1. Preheat the slow cooker to Low.
2. Lightly coat the bottom of a sauté pan with olive oil. Brown the short ribs over medium heat, in batches if necessary, until browned and caramelized. Transfer the ribs to the slow cooker insert.
3. Add the onions to the sauté pan and turn the heat to medium-low. Cook the onions until they are very limp and lightly browned, about 15 minutes. Add the garlic and cook for 5 minutes more. Add the onion mixture and chicken stock to the ribs. Cover the slow cooker and cook on Low for 8 hours.
4. Remove the meat and onions from the slow cooker and cool. Drain the liquid from the meat and place in the refrigerator to allow the fat to rise to the top. Skim off and discard the fat.
5. Shred the meat with your hands and discard the fat, bones, and membranes. Run the meat and onions through a meat grinder with a medium blade or pulse in a food processor. (I like my kreplach meat to have a little texture to it and not be pasty.)

Combine the ground mixture and skimmed liquid in a sauté pan and cook over medium-high heat until the mixture is only slightly moist. Season with salt and pepper.

6. Line a sheet pan with parchment paper. If using wonton skins, cut them into 2½-inch squares. Working in batches, lay out the kreplach dough or wonton squares on a lightly floured work surface. Lightly brush the squares with water. Place a teaspoon of meat in the center of the square and fold over to form a triangle. Push out any air bubbles and press the edges together to seal. Place the kreplach on the sheet pan. The kreplach can be frozen at this point and stored in a heavy freezer bag for up to 3 months.

7. To cook the kreplach, bring a large pot of water to a boil. Boil the kreplach until they float to the top, about 5 minutes. With a slotted spoon or wire skimmer, transfer the kreplach to a sheet pan. Add the kreplach to your favorite soup right before serving.

KREPLACH DOUGH

MAKES ENOUGH DOUGH
FOR 75 KREPLACH

2 cups all-purpose flour
2 eggs
1 tablespoon water
½ teaspoon kosher salt

1. Place the flour on a clean work surface and make a well in the center.

2. Whisk the eggs with the water and salt. Pour the egg mixture into the center of the well. Work the eggs into the flour a little at a time until the mixture forms a ball of dough. Push the excess flour to the side and add more if the dough feels sticky.

3. Knead the dough until smooth and elastic, about 5 minutes. Wrap the dough in plastic wrap and rest it in the refrigerator for up to 1 day.

4. Cut the dough into small sections, about the size of a golf ball. Keeping the rest of the dough covered, flatten one piece dough and feed it into a pasta machine set at number 5. Flour the dough lightly and lower the pasta machine to number 4. Feed the dough through the machine. Continue until the dough has gone through the machine setting at number 1. Place the rolled dough on a lightly floured baking sheet and cover with a clean towel.

5. Continue rolling the rest of the dough until all the dough has gone through the machine to the lowest setting. Cut the dough into 2½-inch squares. Place the cut dough on parchment paper–lined baking sheets and cover with a slightly damp towel to keep the dough from drying out and cracking.

PAREVE

MUSHROOM TERRINE

MEAT

MAKES 6 CUPS

This dressy terrine makes a great appetizer or first course. It is very earthy and fragrant, and delicious served on a bed of baby greens drizzled with a balsamic dressing or pomegranate molasses. For a beautiful presentation, place the terrine on a cake pedestal and surround it with homemade crackers and flat breads.

3½ cups Essential Chicken Stock
    (page 207) or Veal Stock (page 210)
1 ounce (¼ cup) dried porcini mushrooms
Olive oil
4 ounces fresh cremini mushrooms with
    stems, sliced
Kosher salt and freshly ground black
    pepper
¾ cup minced shallots
2 garlic cloves, minced
3 cups Mushroom Duxelles (page 214)
¼ cup dry sherry
4 large eggs
¼ cup (1 ounce) whole unblanched
    almonds, toasted (see page 199) and
    finely ground in a food processor
¼ cup chopped fresh flat-leaf parsley
2 tablespoons chopped fresh thyme

⅓ cup fine fresh bread crumbs (leftover
    challah works well for this)
1½ tablespoons fresh lemon juice

1. Place 1½ cups of the chicken stock in a small saucepan and add the porcini mushrooms. Bring the mixture to a boil and turn down to simmer for 5 minutes. Remove from the heat and allow the mixture to cool.

2. Remove the porcini mushrooms and set aside. Add the remaining stock to the mushroom liquid. Return to the heat and reduce until the liquid measures 1 cup.

3. Lightly coat the bottom of a sauté pan with olive oil. Sauté the cremini mushrooms in batches until lightly browned with crispy edges, 8 to 10 minutes. Add more oil as necessary. Season each batch with salt and pepper and set aside.

4. Sauté the shallots and garlic until they are very soft but not browned.

5. Combine the mushroom duxelles in a food processor with the porcini mushrooms, the shallot mixture, sherry, eggs, almonds, parsley, thyme, bread crumbs, and lemon juice. Process until thoroughly pureed. Stir in the sautéed mushrooms.

6 Line an 8½ × 4½ × 2½–inch terrine with plastic wrap. Pour the mushroom mixture into the terrine and cover the top tightly with plastic wrap. Fill the insert with 2 inches of water to create a water bath for poaching the terrine. Place the terrine in the slow cooker insert. Cover and cook for 2 hours on High, until the terrine is set and a toothpick comes out clean but still moist.

7 Remove the terrine and chill overnight or at least 4 hours. Unmold and remove the plastic wrap before serving.

PEPERONATA WITH CROSTINI

PAREVE

MAKES 4 CUPS PEPERONATA

This tempting concoction of peppers, onions, and sweet garlic is as fragrant as it is beautiful. On a recent trip to the farmers' market, I was drawn in by the mountains of red, yellow, orange, and purple peppers. They were long, round, unevenly shaped, and everything in between—I wish I'd had my camera with me. Instead, I stuffed my bag full and rushed home with my treasure. Several hours later I had a gorgeous bowl of creamy pepper stew.

My family ate the peperonata on garlicky crostini, drizzled with olive oil, as an antipasto. We also gobbled it up several nights later tossed with pasta and mounded on grilled steaks. Basically, you can spread it on everything. Serve the peperonata at room temperature or slightly warmed in a low oven.

Buy the ripest peppers you can find. The flavor will be rich and deep. The peperonata can be stored, covered, in the refrigerator for up to 3 days, or frozen for up to 3 months. Because the raw peppers are bulky, you will need a 6½-quart slow cooker for this recipe.

FOR THE PEPERONATA

3 pounds peppers, preferably a mix of sweet and slightly spicy red, orange, and yellow peppers, stemmed, seeded, and thinly sliced

2 large sweet onions, very thinly sliced

8 large garlic cloves, very thinly sliced

1 small handful of thyme sprigs

2 tablespoons sugar

2 tablespoons balsamic vinegar

1 teaspoon chili flakes (optional)

¼ cup torn fresh basil leaves

¼ cup olive oil

Kosher salt and freshly ground black pepper

FOR THE CROSTINI

1 baguette sliced on the diagonal into ½-inch slices

Olive oil

1 whole peeled garlic clove

SUGGESTED GARNISHES

Basil leaves, grated Parmesan cheese

1. **Make the Peperonata.** Preheat a 6½-quart slow cooker to High. Place the peppers, onions, garlic, thyme sprigs, sugar, vinegar, chili flakes (if using), basil, and olive oil in the slow cooker insert. Cover and cook on High for 2 hours. Lower the heat and cook on Low for another 4 hours, until the peppers are very soft and almost melted in texture.

2. Remove the thyme stems (the leaves will have fallen off) and adjust the seasoning with salt and pepper.

3. **Make the Crostini.** While the peppers cook, preheat the oven to 400°F.

4. Lay the baguette slices on a sheet pan. Lightly brush the slices with olive oil. Toast the bread in the oven until crispy and lightly browned.

5. Allow the toasted bread to cool. Rub each slice with the garlic clove.

6. Mound about 1 heaping tablespoon of the peperonata on each crostini and garnish with basil leaves or sprinkle with grated Parmesan cheese.

TONGUE SALAD
WITH HORSERADISH AÏOLI

MAKES 6 TO 8 SERVINGS

If you have never tried beef tongue, this is a perfect starting place. Or perhaps you already love it; plenty of people do, because this has been one of my more popular menu items for years. The texture of this inexpensive meat is succulent and the flavor is rich and "beefy." Braised tongue is common on many ethnic menus including French, Italian, Eastern European, and Spanish. The simple ingredients complement the flavor without covering it up. This Spanish tapas version of tongue is perfect as a first-course appetizer or salad.

I like to serve it as a light dinner or Shabbat lunch, but it is also perfect for a Passover lunch or any time of the year.

FOR THE TONGUE

One 3-pound tongue
1 large Spanish onion, chopped
1 medium carrot, peeled and chopped

1 whole head of garlic, cut in half horizontally
1 bay leaf
Several thyme sprigs
Several parsley sprigs
6 whole black peppercorns (about ¼ teaspoon)
Olive oil

FOR THE SALAD

2 medium beets
Neutral-flavored oil such as canola
4 cups frisée or other hearty lettuce torn into pieces
1 large fennel bulb, trimmed and thinly sliced
2 celery stalks, thinly sliced
2 medium carrots, peeled and thinly sliced
1 medium red onion, peeled and thinly sliced
Horseradish Aïoli (page 185)

1. **Make the Tongue.** Preheat the slow cooker to Low. Place the tongue, onion, carrot, garlic, bay leaf, thyme, parsley, and peppercorns into the slow cooker insert. Add water to cover. Cover and cook on Low for 4 to 5 hours. Remove the tongue from the liquid and set aside to cool. Discard the cooking liquid.

2. When the tongue is cool, peel off the outer skin and trim away the fatty underside.

3. Place a large sauté pan over medium heat. Lightly coat the bottom of the pan with olive oil. Brown the tongue on all sides. Refrigerate the tongue until it is completely cool.

4. **Make the Salad.** While the tongue is cooking, preheat the oven to 350°F. Coat the beets lightly with oil, wrap in aluminum foil, and roast for 1 hour or until a knife pierces them easily. Remove from the oven and let cool. When cool, slip off the skins and slice the beets into about ½-inch rounds.

5. Place the frisée on a platter. Arrange the beets, fennel, celery, carrots, and onion on the frisée. Thinly slice the tongue and arrange the slices on top of the vegetables. Dollop some of the aïoli on top of the meat. Pass additional aïoli on the side.

VARIATION

When I serve tongue as an appetizer, I like to slice the meat very thin and serve it mounded up on crusty bread with a creamy, tangy horse-radish sauce.

Soups

Soup puts the heart at ease, calms down the violence of hunger, eliminates the tension of the day, and awakens and refines the appetite.
—AUGUSTE ESCOFFIER

*T*here is nothing more reassuring to me during a long day at work than knowing I have a big batch of soup cooking at home. All of a sudden, the traffic, endless errands, phone calls, and even bad weather seem a little less burdensome. In fact, knowing that my slow cooker has picked up the preparation where I left off makes me almost giddy—and definitely excited for dinner.

My love of soup started as a child, watching my father enthusiastically poking around in cabinets and the refrigerator looking for the perfect soup ingredients. I am not sure he ever knew how his soup was going to turn out, but he certainly enjoyed creating his masterpieces and presenting them to us, his devoted fans. When the weather was miserable or if someone in the house was ill, you could find my father in the kitchen, chopping and stirring his way to the perfect antidote (he was a pharmacist, after all). I was often the appointed sous chef and cherished those opportunities to spend time with him. Amazingly, we would start with some simple ingredients and a few embellishments—a couple of songs, some jokes—and shortly thereafter we had a big pot of warm, welcoming soup.

I still share my father's adoration for fussing over a pot of from-scratch soup. But I rarely have the time or energy after a long day on my feet cooking at work to come home and begin again. This is where my love affair with my slow cooker began. With some simple organization and preparation, I can come home to the big flavor and gorgeous texture of a slow-cooked soup like Tomato and Basmati Rice Soup (page 48) or Curried Split Pea Soup (page 44) that I otherwise would have never had the time to prepare.

My equation for great soup starts with great ingredients. Like my father, I choose my elements carefully. First I decide if I am having dairy or meat. Next, I "check the calendar," turning to the produce department or local farmers' market to tell me what vegetables are in season and at peak flavor and abundance. (A zucchini that has spent days on a truck to arrive in the Midwest is not going to be a tasty addition to my pot. On the other hand, a zucchini that has spent only an hour or so to arrive at my local farmers' market is going to be at its zenith of flavor.) Finally, I let my tongue and taste buds take over. There are pureed soups with creamy, rich textures like Cauliflower-Apple Soup (page 56) with the embellishment of duck confit, and soups comprised of rich homemade stock with chunks of vegetables like Pasta e Fagioli (page 49). I love both types—I just let my mood decide.

Once I have decided what type of soup I want to make, I start planning ahead. A great soup does require a bit of effort, and while the slow cooker will do the lion's share of the work, it's important to help the process along. Vegetables should be cut to the same size to ensure each ingredient will cook at about the same rate. The vegetables and meat should also be browned before going into the slow cooker. This process of caramelizing the natural sugars deepens the flavors of vegetables and meats, gives them a gorgeous toasty color, and flavors the broth. For tips on browning, see page 6.

As Dad taught me, a good pot of soup is something to really rave about. The combination of great ingredients and some tender loving care can yield an amazing meal that will have your family asking for more.

CHICK PEA AND LENTIL SOUP

MAKES 6 SERVINGS

This savory soup is perfect for cold nights. I think it is perfectly delicious pareve and we eat it that way often as a first course or vegetarian main dish. With the addition of Spicy Chicken Meatballs (page 112) or diced leftover Rubbed Brisket (page 64), the soup becomes a hearty main course. Made with water, it becomes a pareve starter for any type of meal.

Olive oil

3 medium carrots, peeled and diced small

3 celery stalks, diced small

1 large Spanish onion, diced small

1 medium fennel bulb, trimmed and diced small

3 garlic cloves, chopped

2 cups red lentils or green lentils (see Sources, page 233)

1 cup dried chick peas, soaked overnight and drained, or two 15-ounce cans, drained

One 28-ounce can whole peeled plum tomatoes with their juices, crushed (see page 8)

2 teaspoons ground coriander

1 teaspoon ground cumin

3 tablespoons fresh lemon juice

2 quarts Essential Chicken Stock (page 207), Vegetable Stock (page 211), or water

Kosher salt and freshly ground black pepper

SUGGESTED GARNISHES

Charmoula (page 187), Harissa (page 181), chopped fresh flat-leaf parsley, chopped cilantro

PAREVE
or Dairy
or Meat

1. Preheat a slow cooker to Low.
2. Place a large sauté pan over medium heat. Lightly coat the bottom of the pan with olive oil. Sauté the carrots, celery, onion, fennel, and garlic, in batches if necessary, until lightly browned. Transfer the vegetables to the slow cooker insert.
3. Add the lentils, chick peas, tomatoes with their juices, coriander, cumin, lemon juice, and chicken stock. Cover and cook on Low for 8 to 9 hours if using dried chick peas or on Low for 4 hours if using canned chick peas.
4. Before serving, adjust the seasoning with salt and pepper. Serve this soup out of a pretty tureen and pass the garnishes in small bowls.

TORTILLA SOUP

PAREVE
or Dairy
or Meat

MAKES 6 SERVINGS

This Tex-Mex classic is a meal in a bowl and one of my son Zach's favorite soups. I like to add lots of vegetables and to float a smoky chipotle chile in it to add depth. This soup is vegetarian (pareve). You can garnish it with cheese and sour cream, which would fit a dairy meal, or you can make it a meat recipe by adding chicken or turkey instead.

Olive oil

2 medium Spanish onions, chopped

2 red bell peppers, roasted (see page 37), stemmed, seeded, peeled, and diced

1 poblano chile, roasted (see page 37), stemmed, seeded, peeled, and diced

Kosher salt and freshly ground black pepper

3 garlic cloves, finely diced

1 chipotle chile (see Note)

1 tablespoon Ancho Chile Powder (page 200, or see Sources, page 233)

½ teaspoon ground cumin

½ teaspoon ground coriander

3 tablespoons tomato paste

6 ripe fresh, tomatoes, seeded and chopped, or one 28-ounce can whole peeled plum tomatoes, drained (juice reserved) and crushed (see page 8)

2 quarts Vegetable Stock (page 211)

3 fresh corn tortillas

1 cup corn kernels (frozen works well for this)

½ cup green beans cut into bite-sized pieces (frozen works well for this)

Kosher salt and freshly ground black pepper

SUGGESTED GARNISHES

Chef Laura's Famous Guacamole (page 20), chopped fresh cilantro, fresh lime juice, shredded sharp Cheddar cheese, crumbled goat cheese, sour cream, shredded cooked chicken or turkey

1. Preheat a 6½-quart (or smaller) slow cooker to Low.

2. Place a large sauté pan over medium heat. Lightly coat the bottom of the pan with oil. Brown the onions and peppers in batches. Season each batch with salt and pepper. Add the garlic to the last batch of vegetables at the end to avoid overbrowning. Transfer the vegetables to the slow cooker insert.

3. Add the chipotle chile, ancho chile powder, cumin, coriander, tomato paste, tomatoes (with their juices), and stock. Cover and cook on Low for 6 hours.

4. Toast the tortillas over the open flame of a gas burner or in a dry cast-iron pan, until they are browned in spots and smell of toasted corn. Break up the tortillas into small pieces and add them, the corn kernels, and green beans to the slow cooker.

5. Cover and cook on High for 1 hour.

6. Ladle the soup into bowls and pass your choice of garnishes.

NOTE

▶ Chipotle chiles are smoked jalapeño peppers. They can be found with a hechsher (kosher certification) online (see Sources, page 233).

HOW TO ROAST PEPPERS

Preheat the oven to 400°F. Rub the whole peppers liberally with olive oil—the oil helps the skin blister and separate it from the flesh. Place the peppers on a baking sheet. Roast the peppers in the preheated oven until the skin is very dark, about 20 minutes. Remove the peppers and place them in a bowl. Cover the bowl with plastic and allow the peppers to cool completely. Remove the stem, shake out the seeds, and peel off the skin with your fingers or by rubbing lightly with a paper towel. Do not rinse it off under running water (you'll lose a lot of flavor that way). The peeled peppers can be stored in the refrigerator, covered, for up to 1 week. Roasted peppers can be also stored in the refrigerator, covered with olive oil, for up to 3 months. The oil can be used for sautéing and making vinaigrettes.

BLACK BEAN SOUP

PAREVE
or Dairy
or Meat

MAKES 6 SERVINGS

I like to make this hearty soup vegetarian and to top it with sour cream. However, you can easily add shredded cooked chicken or turkey before serving the soup and skip the sour cream. The addition of a chipotle chile does add some heat and a complex smoky fragrance and flavor. Remove the chipotle before serving.

Olive oil

1 large Spanish onion, chopped

1 large red bell pepper, seeded and cut into medium dice

2 garlic cloves, chopped

One 28-ounce can whole peeled plum tomatoes with their juices, crushed (see page 8)

½ cup Sofrito (page 215)

1 teaspoon ground cumin

1 tablespoon ground coriander

2 teaspoons pimenton (see Note, page 59)

2 tablespoons tomato paste

5 cups Vegetable Stock (page 211) or water

2 cups dried black beans, sorted through, soaked overnight, and drained

Kosher salt and freshly ground black pepper

SUGGESTED GARNISHES

Chopped fresh cilantro, fresh lime juice, chopped fresh flat-leaf parsley, sour cream, grated cheese, shredded cooked chicken or turkey

1. Preheat a slow cooker to High.
2. Place a medium sauté pan over medium-high heat. Lightly coat the bottom of the pan with oil. Cook the onion, stirring occasionally, until soft and brown, about 10 minutes. Add the red pepper and garlic. Continue cooking until the pepper has softened, about 5 minutes. Transfer the mixture to the slow cooker insert.
3. Add the tomatoes with their juices, sofrito, cumin, coriander, pimenton, tomato paste, stock, and beans to the insert. Stir to combine. Cover and cook on High for 4 hours, until the beans are soft.
4. Remove 1 cup of the beans and process in a food processor until they are very creamy. Add the pureed beans back to the soup. Adjust the seasoning with salt and pepper.
5. Ladle the soup into bowls. Pass small bowls of garnishes and let everyone customize his or her own soup.

CREAMY TOMATO SOUP

MAKES 6 SERVINGS

My family eats a lot of tomato soup in our house, probably owing to my obsession with "all things tomato." I use a sharp white Cheddar cheese, which lends this soup a comforting creaminess. You can also use a smoked Cheddar or Muenster for a deep, earthy flavor. I like to add playful garnishes to this soup like my Rosemary and Parmesan Popcorn (page 22) or shredded cheese.

4 tablespoons (½ stick) unsalted butter

2 large shallots, finely minced

3 tablespoons all-purpose flour

One 28-ounce can whole peeled plum tomatoes with their juices, crushed (see page 8)

One 28-ounce can tomato puree

2 tablespoons tomato paste

1½ cups whole milk

½ cup heavy cream or half-and-half

2 cups shredded sharp Cheddar cheese (½ pound)

Kosher salt and freshly ground black pepper

SUGGESTED GARNISHES
Rosemary and Parmesan Popcorn (page 22) or Parmesan Crisps (page 21)

1. Preheat a slow cooker to Low.
2. Melt the butter in a medium sauté pan over medium-low heat. Add the shallots and cook until the shallots are very soft and translucent, about 10 minutes. Add the flour and increase the heat to medium. Stir to combine until the mixture forms a loose paste.
3. Add the canned tomatoes with their juices and stir thoroughly to combine. Transfer the mixture to the slow cooker insert. Add the tomato puree and paste. Stir to combine. Cover and cook on Low for 2 hours.
4. Add the milk, cream, and cheese. Stir to combine. Cover and cook for 1 hour longer. Add more milk if necessary to adjust the consistency. Season with salt and pepper.
5. Ladle the soup into bowls and pass the garnishes.

VEGETARIAN CHILI

PAREVE
or Dairy

MAKES 8 SERVINGS

Chili is the perfect accompaniment for Sunday game day or a movie night. I turned a dish that could be ordinary into something extraordinary by combining different types of beans, vegetables, and peppers for layers of flavor. My family serves it steaming hot, right out of the slow cooker, accompanied by a platter filled with lots of tempting accompaniments. Adding cheese or sour cream will make it dairy.

For great taste and visual effect, use all the different beans I do or a combination of what you have on hand or like. The squash, sweet potatoes, and a variety of peppers make this hearty dish delicious and nutritious. If you prefer a milder chili, add the smoky chipotle later in the cooking process so less heat will flavor the chili.

4 cups dried beans (pinto beans, kidney beans, black beans, and/or chick peas), sorted through and soaked overnight

Neutral-flavored oil such as canola

2 large red onions, peeled and diced

1 small butternut squash, peeled, seeded, and cut into large dice

1 large sweet potato, peeled and cut into large dice

Kosher salt and freshly ground black pepper

6 garlic cloves, minced

2 red bell peppers, roasted (see page 37), stemmed, seeded, peeled, and diced

2 dried ancho chiles, stemmed, seeded, toasted (see page 40), and torn into small pieces

1 chipotle chile (optional; see Note)

1 tablespoon ground cumin

1 tablespoon ground coriander

6 tablespoons tomato paste

One 28- to 29-ounce can tomato puree

One 28-ounce can whole peeled plum tomatoes with their juices

7 cups water

SUGGESTED ACCOMPANIMENTS

Fresh or thawed frozen corn kernels (cooked), chopped scallions, grated Cheddar cheese, tortilla chips, sour cream, chopped red onions, chopped jalapeños, chopped fresh flat-leaf parsley, chopped fresh cilantro, fresh lime wedges, shaved bittersweet chocolate

1. Preheat a slow cooker to Low.

2. Drain the beans, rinse them under cold water, and set aside.

3. Place a large sauté pan over medium-high heat. Lightly coat the bottom of the pan with oil. Brown the onions, squash, and sweet potato in batches. Season each batch with salt and pepper. Transfer the vegetables to the slow cooker insert.

4. Turn the heat to medium and lightly sauté the garlic and roasted peppers until golden. Add to the insert.

5. Add the drained beans, the ancho chiles, chipotle (if using), cumin, coriander, tomato paste, tomato puree, tomatoes with their juices, and water to the slow cooker. Cover and cook on Low for 6 to 8 hours until the beans are tender. Remove the chipotle chile before serving.

6. Ladle into bowls and pass your choice of garnishes.

NOTE

▶ Chipotle chiles are smoked jalapeño peppers. They can be found with a hechsher (kosher certification) online (see Sources, page 233).

HOW TO PREPARE ANCHO CHILES

Remove the stem by breaking it off with your hands and shake out the seeds. Hold the ancho with tongs over a low flame until it has darkened and smells toasty, about 30 seconds.

RIBOLLITA

PAREVE
or Dairy
or Meat

MAKES 8 SERVINGS

The name of this hearty Tuscan soup means "twice boiled." Traditionally, it was made from leftover minestrone soup combined with stale bread to create a new dish. I break with tradition by adding the toasted bread toward the end of cooking. I also like to add a Parmesan cheese rind to the stock, which adds a refined richness to the dish. I save the rinds from Parmesan cheese in a bag in my freezer. Anytime I need an extra boost of flavor, in go the rinds.

Serve this soup with chunks of garlicky toast to contrast with the creamy beans.

2 cups dried cannellini beans, sorted
    through, rinsed, and soaked
    overnight
Olive oil
1 medium red onion, chopped
1 small leek, white part only, chopped
4 medium carrots, peeled and sliced
4 medium zucchini, trimmed and sliced
3 garlic cloves, chopped, plus 1 whole
    peeled garlic clove

1 small head savoy cabbage (about 2
    pounds), shredded
1 bunch cavolo nero (see Note) or kale
    (about 1 pound)
1 bunch Swiss chard (about 1 pound),
    shredded
4 medium Idaho or russet potatoes,
    peeled and cut into ½-inch dice
1 cup cut green beans in bite-sized pieces
    (fresh or frozen)
One 28-ounce can whole peeled plum
    tomatoes with their juices, crushed
    (see page 8)
¼ cup tomato paste
Bouquet garni consisting of 6 thyme
    sprigs, 6 flat-leaf parsley sprigs,
    and 1 bay leaf, tied together with
    kitchen twine
6 cups Vegetable Stock (page 211) or
    water
Parmesan cheese rind (optional)
Four 1-inch-thick slices stale Italian bread,
    toasted

SUGGESTED GARNISHES

Extra-virgin olive oil, grated Parmesan cheese

1. Preheat a slow cooker to Low.

2. Drain and rinse the soaked beans. Place the beans into the slow cooker insert.

3. Place a large sauté pan over medium heat. Lightly coat the bottom of the pan with olive oil. Sauté the onion, leek, carrots, and zucchini in batches until the vegetables are lightly browned. Transfer the vegetables to the slow cooker insert.

4. Add the chopped garlic, savoy cabbage, cavolo nero, chard, potatoes, green beans, tomatoes with their juices, tomato paste, bouquet garni, vegetable stock, and cheese rind, if using, to the insert. Cover and cook on Low for 6 hours, until the cannellini beans are creamy and barely holding together.

5. Rub the toasted bread with the garlic clove. Place the toasted bread on top of the soup. Press down lightly on it. Cover and cook for 30 minutes more.

6. Mix the bread into the soup before serving. Serve the soup in bowls, drizzled with olive oil and sprinkled with grated Parmesan cheese.

NOTE

▶ Cavolo nero translates to "black kale" in Italian. This variety of cabbage does not form heads but rather looks like a bunch of big dark green or purplish-black leaves. Cavolo nero can be found in some specialty stores, but if it is not available in your area, you can substitute Swiss chard, another kale, or any hearty braising green.

CURRIED SPLIT PEA SOUP

PAREVE
or Dairy
or Meat

MAKES 6 SERVINGS

Common pea soup becomes exotic with the addition of curry. I like the way this soup satisfies my craving for a little richness and spice without a lot of fuss. I always brown the vegetables in small batches. It is important to brown all the vegetables on all sides. This extra step ensures deep flavor and a natural sweetness from the caramelized sugars.

Overcrowding the pan results in the vegetables steaming and will actually prevent them from browning. This recipe has very few ingredients, so you want to maximize the flavor of each of them.

This soup actually gets better the second day, so make it a day ahead of when you plan to serve it, or set some aside for leftovers. You could make pareve batches dairy by garnishing with yogurt. You could make a meat version with chicken stock.

Olive oil

3 medium carrots, peeled and diced small

1 large red onion, diced small

1 pound new potatoes, scrubbed but not peeled, diced small

2 garlic cloves, chopped

Kosher salt and freshly ground black pepper

2 cups dried green split peas

3 tablespoons Curry Powder (page 198)

6 cups Vegetable Stock (page 211) or Essential Chicken Stock (page 207)

SUGGESTED GARNISHES
Plain yogurt (if using vegetable stock)

1 Preheat a slow cooker to Low.

2 Place a large sauté pan over medium heat. Lightly coat the bottom of the pan with olive oil. Sauté the carrots, onion, potatoes, and garlic in batches until lightly browned. Season each batch with salt and pepper. Do not overbrown the garlic. Transfer the vegetables to the slow cooker insert.

3 Add the split peas, curry powder, and stock to the insert. Stir to combine. Cover and cook on Low for 6 hours.

4 Adjust the seasoning with salt and pepper. Ladle the soup into bowls. Serve with yogurt, if desired.

ONION SOUP

MAKES 6 SERVINGS

This remake of the classic French soup tastes smooth and full-flavored from its long cooking in the slow cooker. Good-quality cheese makes a big difference. The availability of fine kosher cheeses has grown considerably in the United States, but they are not yet carried by all grocery stores. Search online and experiment until you find what you like.

4 tablespoons (½ stick) unsalted butter

2 large Spanish onions, cut in half and very thinly sliced

2 garlic cloves, chopped, plus 1 whole peeled garlic clove

2 teaspoons all-purpose flour

3 thyme sprigs

½ teaspoon freshly grated nutmeg

2 bay leaves

¾ cup dry white wine such as chardonnay

1 quart Vegetable Stock (page 211)

1½ cups water

Six ½-inch-thick diagonal baguette slices

1 cup shredded Gruyère or Swiss cheese

2 tablespoons finely grated Parmesan cheese, preferably Parmigiano-Reggiano

Kosher salt and freshly ground black pepper

1. Preheat a slow cooker to High.

2. Melt the butter in a large sauté pan over medium heat. Add the onions and cook slowly until the onions are very soft and lightly caramelized, about 20 minutes. Add the garlic at the end of the cooking and cook for 5 minutes more.

3. Add the flour and stir over the heat for 3 minutes. Transfer the mixture to the slow cooker insert. Add the thyme, nutmeg, bay leaves, wine, stock, and water. Cover and cook on High for 4 hours.

4. Preheat the oven to 400°F. Line a baking sheet with foil or parchment paper.

5. Just before serving, place the baguette slices on the baking sheet. Toast the baguette slices in the oven until they are lightly browned and crispy. Remove from the oven and allow them to cool slightly.

6. Rub the slices with the garlic clove. Divide the shredded cheese among the baguette slices. Sprinkle evenly with the Parmesan cheese. Place the baguette slices back in the oven and cook until the cheese has melted and is lightly browned.

7. Adjust the seasoning with salt and pepper. Divide the soup among the serving bowls and top each bowl with a baguette slice.

MULLIGATAWNY

**PAREVE
or Dairy**

MAKES 6 SERVINGS

The literal translation for mulligatawny is "pepper water." The smoky mixture of curry and turmeric in this version helps it live up to its name.

At first glance the list of ingredients may seem a bit lengthy. However, this soup is a snap to put together. Curry leaves are not used to make curry powder but are used in many Indian dishes. Curry leaves can be found at Indian grocery stores and in the produce section of many grocery stores. They are used in the same manner in Indian cuisine as bay leaves are used in this country. These aromatic leaves have a citrus aroma that scents broths and this delicious soup. Basil leaves are a good substitute if you can't find curry leaves. Chick pea flour is used as a thickener for this soup; it also adds nutrients and a bit of flavor. It is commonly found in many grocery stores and health food markets. Garnishing with yogurt makes it dairy.

1 medium red onion, chopped

2 medium carrots, peeled and diced

2 medium Idaho or russet potatoes, peeled and diced

2 small turnips, peeled and diced

Olive oil

Kosher salt and freshly ground black pepper

4 garlic cloves, coarsely chopped

2 tablespoons Curry Powder (page 198)

½ teaspoon ground turmeric

1½ tablespoons chick pea flour (optional; see Sources, page 233)

6 cups Vegetable Stock (page 211)

12 fresh curry leaves (see Sources, page 233) or 8 fresh basil leaves

One 28-ounce can whole peeled plum tomatoes with their juices, crushed (see page 8)

1 tablespoon grated peeled fresh ginger

One 13.5- to 14-ounce can unsweetened coconut milk

1 cup red lentils (see Sources, page 233)

Lime wedges, chopped cilantro, chopped fresh flat-leaf parsley, plain yogurt

1. Preheat a slow cooker to Low.
2. Brown the onion, carrots, potatoes, and turnips in batches over medium-high heat in a sauté pan lightly coated with olive oil. Season each batch with salt and pepper. Transfer the vegetables to the slow cooker insert.
3. Add the garlic, curry powder, turmeric, chick pea flour, stock, curry leaves, tomatoes with their juices, ginger, coconut milk, and lentils to the insert. Cover and cook on Low for 4 to 5 hours or on High for 3 hours until the lentils are creamy.
4. Adjust the seasoning with salt and pepper. Ladle the soup into bowls or in a tureen and pass the garnishes.

TOMATO AND
BASMATI RICE SOUP

MEAT
or Pareve

MAKES 6 SERVINGS

I could eat this soup every day. This particular version, one of my favorites, tastes a bit more exotic than the standard cream of tomato. The spices and fragrant basmati rice lend a perfumed quality and the natural starch from the rice makes the soup rich, thick, and creamy. For a full-flavored pareve version, use vegetable stock.

Olive oil

1 medium Spanish onion, diced

2 medium carrots, peeled and diced

1 large fennel bulb, trimmed and diced
    (reserve the fronds for garnish)

Kosher salt and freshly ground black
    pepper

3 garlic cloves, minced

2 tablespoons Moroccan Spice Mix (page
    201)

Two 28-ounce cans whole peeled plum
    tomatoes with their juices, crushed
    (see page 8)

6 tablespoons tomato paste

6 cups Essential Chicken Stock (page 207)
    or Vegetable Stock (page 211)

1 cup white basmati rice

SUGGESTED GARNISHES
Charmoula (page 187), Harissa (page 181), chopped fresh flat-leaf parsley, chopped cilantro

1. Preheat a slow cooker to Low.

2. Place a large sauté pan over medium-high heat. Lightly coat the bottom of the pan with olive oil. Brown the onion, carrots, and fennel in batches over medium heat. Season each batch with salt and pepper.

3. Add the garlic to the last batch of vegetables and lightly sauté it for 2 minutes more. Transfer the vegetables to the slow cooker insert.

4. Add the Moroccan Spice Mix, canned tomatoes and their juices, tomato paste, stock, and rice. Cover and cook on Low for 4 hours. Add more stock if the soup gets too thick. Adjust the seasoning with salt and pepper.

5. Ladle the soup into bowls and pass the garnishes.

PASTA E FAGIOLI

MAKES 6 SERVINGS

This Italian classic (pasta and beans) is a great example of how you can make a simple, delicious meal out of pantry staples. For this dish (and many others) using the right bean is essential—I prefer borlotti beans, which have a firm texture and sweet nutty flavor that pairs well with the soft pasta. However, if you cannot find borlotti beans, cranberry beans also work well.

1½ cups dried borlotti beans or cranberry beans, sorted through and soaked overnight

Olive oil

1 pound ground beef

1 large Spanish onion, chopped

3 garlic cloves, finely chopped

3 tablespoons tomato paste

One 14- to 15-ounce can whole peeled plum tomatoes with their juices, crushed (see page 8)

1 teaspoon dried oregano

6 thyme sprigs

1 cup small pasta shells or other small shape

6 cups Essential Chicken Stock (page 207)

Kosher salt and freshly ground black pepper

SUGGESTED GARNISHES

Extra-virgin olive oil, chopped fresh herbs (flat-leaf parsley, oregano, thyme, basil)

1. Preheat a slow cooker to Low.
2. Drain and rinse the beans. Place the beans into the slow cooker insert.
3. Place a large sauté pan over medium heat. Lightly coat the bottom of the pan with olive oil. Brown the meat, breaking up any large clumps. With a slotted spoon, transfer the meat to the slow cooker insert.
4. Drain all but 1 tablespoon of fat out of the sauté pan. Add the onion to the sauté pan. Cook, stirring occasionally, until the onion is lightly colored and soft, about 10 minutes. Add the garlic to the pan and cook for 3 minutes more.
5. Add the onion mixture, the tomato paste, tomatoes with their juices, oregano, thyme, pasta, and chicken stock to the insert. Stir to combine, cover, and cook on Low for 6 hours, until the beans are tender.
6. Remove the thyme stems. Season to taste with salt and pepper. Ladle the soup into bowls. Drizzle each bowl of soup with extra-virgin olive oil and sprinkle with herbs.

SWEET-AND-SOUR CABBAGE SOUP

MAKES 6 SERVINGS

The beets in this soup turn it an incredibly gorgeous scarlet color, so don't even think of leaving them out. Serve with a loaf of crusty bread and you have a comforting supper. I like to make a big batch and freeze it to eat again on a cold night.

Olive oil

1 pound beef chuck or stew meat, minced very fine

2 large Spanish onions, chopped

3 garlic cloves, finely chopped

3 carrots, peeled and grated on the coarse side of a box grater

3 celery stalks, chopped

2 large red beets, peeled and grated on the coarse side of a box grater

One 28-ounce can plum tomatoes with their juices, crushed (see page 8)

2 tablespoons tomato paste

⅓ cup vinegar, preferably rice vinegar

½ cup sugar

2 quarts Essential Chicken Stock (page 207)

1 large head green cabbage (about 3 pounds), quartered, cored, and very thinly sliced

Kosher salt and freshly ground black pepper

1. Preheat a slow cooker to Low.
2. Lightly coat the bottom of a sauté pan with olive oil. Brown the meat over medium heat, stirring occasionally.
3. Add the onions and continue to cook until the onions are translucent and soft, about 5 minutes.
4. Add the garlic and continue to cook for 2 minutes more.
5. Transfer the meat mixture to the slow cooker insert. Add the carrots, celery, beets, tomatoes with their juices, tomato paste, vinegar, sugar, and chicken stock. Cover and cook on Low for 6 hours or on High for 4 hours.
6. Add the cabbage and cook for 1 hour more on High. Adjust the seasoning with salt and pepper. Ladle the soup into bowls.

SENEGALESE PEANUT SOUP

I once had a staff member from Senegal who got teary in his descriptions of peanut soup and begged me to feature it on the menu. I finally made a batch. I must have nailed the flavors and texture of this rich African comfort food, because he asked me to write the recipe for him. I adapted the recipe for the slow cooker and it has been a family favorite ever since.

Brown the vegetables in small batches to ensure big flavor and appealing color and texture. The soup may be cooked two days ahead of serving and can stored, covered, in the refrigerator up to 3 days or frozen for up to 1 month.

Neutral-flavored oil such as canola
1 large sweet potato (about 1 pound), peeled and diced
1 small butternut squash (about 1½ pounds), peeled and diced
2 medium Spanish onions, thinly sliced
3 garlic cloves, minced
Kosher salt and freshly ground black pepper
2 tablespoons Curry Powder (page 198)
1 quart Essential Chicken Stock (page 207)

MEAT

One 14- to 15-ounce can diced tomatoes
2 boneless, skinless chicken breast halves (about 8 ounces), cut into cubes
1 cup creamy peanut butter
1¼ cups unsweetened coconut milk
Kosher salt and freshly ground black pepper

SUGGESTED GARNISHES
Chopped peanuts, chopped scallions, chopped parsley, chopped cilantro

1. Preheat a slow cooker to Low.
2. Place a large sauté pan over medium-high heat. Lightly coat the bottom of the pan with oil. Sauté the sweet potato, squash, onions, and garlic in batches until they are browned, 5 to 7 minutes per batch. Season each batch with salt and pepper. Transfer the vegetables to the slow cooker insert.
3. Add the curry powder, chicken stock, tomatoes with their juices, chicken, and peanut butter to the insert. Stir to combine. Cover and cook on Low for 6 hours.
4. Stir in the coconut milk, cook long enough to heat, and adjust the seasoning with salt and pepper.
5. Ladle the soup into bowls and add your choice of garnishes.

ITALIAN PUMPKIN SOUP

DAIRY

MAKES 8 SERVINGS

There are as many variations of this soup—called crema di zucca *in Italian—as there are shapes of pasta in Italy. I got this recipe from a friend who studied cooking in Tuscany. It is undeniably delicious. This dish makes a great alternative to the more common butternut squash soup. I serve it in on Sukkot (the Jewish harvest holiday), encased in a hollowed-out pumpkin for a dramatic presentation.*

8 cups Vegetable Stock (page 211)

1 ounce (¼ cup) dried porcini mushrooms

Olive oil

One 7-pound sugar pumpkin, peeled, seeded, and diced (about 5 cups), or 3 cups canned pure pumpkin puree (not pumpkin pie mix)

Kosher salt and freshly ground black pepper

12 cipollini onions, peeled (see page 115) and cut in quarters

1 teaspoon freshly grated nutmeg

1 medium head savoy cabbage (about 1½ pounds), quartered, cored, and very thinly sliced

½ cup heavy cream

SUGGESTED GARNISHES

Parmesan Crisps (page 21), ½ cup amaretti crumbs (optional)

1. Place 1 cup of the vegetable stock in a small saucepan with the dried porcini mushrooms. Bring to a simmer. Turn off the heat and set aside.

2. Preheat a slow cooker to Low.

3. If using diced pumpkin, place a large sauté pan over medium-high heat. Lightly coat the bottom of the pan with oil. Brown the pumpkin in batches. Season each batch with salt and pepper. Transfer the pumpkin to the slow cooker insert. If using puree, simply pour it into the slow cooker insert.

4. Sauté the cipollini onions in olive oil (use the same pan, adding more olive oil if necessary) until golden. Transfer the onions to the insert.

5. Pass the soaked mushrooms and their soaking liquid through a strainer to remove any sediment that may be present. Set aside the mushroom pieces and reserve the soaking liquid—it is loaded with flavor.

6. Add the remaining stock, the porcini mushrooms, soaking liquid, and nutmeg to the slow cooker. Cover and cook on Low for 6 hours, until the pumpkin is very soft. If using canned pumpkin puree, cut the cooking time in half.

7. Puree the soup in batches, adding more stock if necessary. Return the soup to the slow cooker.

8. Add the cabbage and the cream to the soup. Cover and cook on High for 1 hour. Adjust the seasoning with salt and pepper.

9. Ladle the soup into bowls and garnish with Parmesan crisps and amaretti crumbs, if using, right before serving.

ROASTED PARSNIP AND JERUSALEM ARTICHOKE SOUP

MEAT

MAKES 6 SERVINGS

The name Jerusalem artichoke is a misnomer. These bumpy tubers are the root of the sunflower plant, which is why they are also called sunchokes. They have a nutty, earthy flavor similar to an artichoke and when paired with sweet roasted parsnips, they are a match made in heaven.

**8 large parsnips (about 3 pounds),
     peeled and cut into large pieces
Olive oil
1 pound Jerusalem artichokes (about 10)
Juice of 1 lemon
3 medium shallots, chopped
2 garlic cloves, chopped
½ cup dry white wine such as chardonnay
2 tablespoons chopped fresh thyme
5 cups Essential Chicken Stock (page 207)
Kosher salt and freshly ground black
     pepper**

SUGGESTED GARNISHES
¼ cup chopped toasted hazelnuts (see page 199), toasted hazelnut oil

1. Preheat the oven to 400°F. Line a baking sheet with parchment paper.
2. Drizzle the parsnip pieces with olive oil. Place the parsnips on the baking sheet. Roast in the oven for 45 minutes, until soft and lightly browned. Transfer the parsnips to the slow cooker insert.
3. While the parsnips are roasting, peel and dice the artichokes. Place the pieces in a bowl of cold water with the lemon juice to keep them from turning dark.
4. Preheat a slow cooker to Low.
5. Place a small sauté pan over medium-high heat. Lightly coat the bottom of the pan with olive oil. Sauté the shallots until they are slightly browned and soft. Add the garlic and cook for 2 minutes more. Add the wine to the pan and cook the mixture for 3 minutes. Add the wine-shallot mixture to the slow cooker insert. Drain the Jerusalem artichoke pieces and add them to the insert. Add the thyme and chicken stock to the insert.
6. Cover and cook on Low for 5 hours, until the Jerusalem artichokes and parsnips are very soft.
7. Puree the soup in batches or with an immersion blender until the soup is very creamy. Season with salt and pepper.
8. Ladle the soup into bowls and garnish with chopped toasted hazelnuts and a drizzle of toasted hazelnut oil.

WILD RICE AND TURKEY CHOWDER

MAKES 8 SERVINGS

I love any recipe that uses wild rice. With a rich, nutty aroma and hearty texture, wild rice is the perfect cold weather addition to soups and stews. This recipe uses leftover turkey, but I think the soup is so heavenly fragrant with mushrooms and herbs that you will want to make turkey just as an excuse to make the soup.

Several tablespoons of turkey pan drippings or olive oil

3 medium celery stalks, diced

2 medium carrots, peeled and diced

8 ounces mushrooms, stems included, chopped

I large Spanish onion, diced

1 cup dry white wine (I prefer chardonnay)

1 ounce (¼ cup) dried porcini mushrooms

2 cups wild rice

1 cup white basmati rice

5 cups Turkey Stock (page 209) or Essential Chicken Stock (page 207)

Bouquet garni of 3 fresh sage leaves, 6 parsley sprigs, 1 bay leaf, and 1 small rosemary sprig, tied together with kitchen twine

2 cups diced cooked turkey

MEAT

SUGGESTED GARNISHES

Chopped fresh flat-leaf parsley, chopped fresh sage

1. Preheat a slow cooker to Low.
2. Place a large sauté pan over medium heat. Lightly coat the bottom of the pan with the turkey drippings or olive oil. Sauté the celery, carrots, mushrooms, and onion in batches until lightly browned. Transfer the vegetables to the slow cooker insert.
3. Add the white wine to the pan and simmer for several minutes. Transfer the wine to the slow cooker insert. Add the porcini mushrooms, wild rice, basmati rice, stock, and bouquet garni to the slow cooker. Stir to combine. Cover and cook on Low for 5 hours, until the wild rice has split open and softened.
4. Remove 2 cups of the soup with rice in it. Puree until creamy. Add the pureed mixture back to the slow cooker and stir to combine. Add the cooked turkey, cover, and cook for 30 minutes more.
5. Remove the bouquet garni. Ladle the soup into bowls and garnish with parsley and sage.

CAULIFLOWER-APPLE SOUP
WITH DUCK CONFIT

MEAT

MAKES 6 SERVINGS

This elegant chilly weather soup makes a perfect first course for a Sukkot (the Jewish harvest holiday) dinner or for any special occasion. The apples and cauliflower combine in style. You could serve the soup ungarnished and enjoy a chic, modern soup or add the duck confit and gild the lily with rich, silky texture and flavor.

The soup can be stored, covered, for up to 3 days, or frozen for up to 1 month. The garnish can be made up to 3 days ahead of serving and reheated in a sauté pan over low heat.

FOR THE SOUP

Olive oil

2 medium Spanish onions, diced

2 garlic cloves, diced

1 large head of cauliflower (about 1½ pounds), trimmed and cut into florets

3 large sweet apples (about 1 pound), such as Honeycrisp, cored, peeled, and diced

½ cup fruity white wine such as chenin blanc

3 tablespoons chopped fresh thyme

5 cups Essential Chicken Stock (page 207)

Kosher salt and freshly ground black pepper

FOR THE DUCK CONFIT

1 teaspoon duck fat or olive oil

⅓ cup shredded Duck Confit (page 122), meat only

1 medium shallot, chopped

2 teaspoons chopped fresh thyme

1 small firm apple such as Honeycrisp, peeled, cored and diced

SUGGESTED GARNISHES

Chopped fresh flat-leaf parsley, chopped fresh thyme

1. **Make the Soup.** Preheat a slow cooker to Low. Place a large sauté pan over medium-low heat. Lightly coat the bottom of the pan with olive oil. Cook the onions, stirring occasionally, until they are very soft and browned, about 20 minutes. Add the garlic and cook for 3 minutes more. Transfer the onions to the slow cooker insert.

2 Lightly recoat the same pan with additional olive oil. Increase the heat to medium. Add the cauliflower and apples to the pan. Cook, stirring occasionally, until the cauliflower and apples are soft and lightly browned, about 10 minutes.

3 Add the wine to the pan. Increase the heat to medium-high and gently scrape up any browned bits (*sucs*; see page 7) with a wooden spatula. Transfer the wine, cauliflower, and apples to the slow cooker insert. Add the thyme and chicken stock. Cover and cook on Low for 5 hours until the cauliflower is very soft.

4 **Make the Duck Confit.** Place a small sauté pan over medium heat. Add the duck fat. Add the shredded duck, shallot, thyme, and apple, and sauté until the apple pieces are lightly browned and soft, about 10 minutes. Keep warm.

5 Puree the soup in batches or use a stick blender. Season the soup with salt and pepper. Ladle the soup into bowls and garnish with a heaping tablespoon of the duck and apple mixture. Sprinkle with the chopped parsley and thyme.

BISON CHILI

MAKES 12 SERVINGS

I originally made this chili with chunks of bison meat, but my customers craved the ground meat texture they grew up with. So I compromised by combining the two and voilà, everyone was happy. I use bison for this recipe due to the meat's sweet and fuller flavor. Most bison are grass-fed and are naturally lower in fat than beef. While beef will work perfectly well, I urge you to look for bison and give it a try (see Sources, page 233).

I like to add Anaheim chiles for a pleasant toasty heat. If you are unsure about chiles, add just a few peppers your first time trying the dish. Most of the heat comes from the seeds and veins inside the chile, so remove those if you prefer a less spicy dish.

In our house, we commonly grate dark chocolate as a garnish for chili. The chocolate is not meant to sweeten the chili, but to heighten the sweetness of the meat and the earthiness of the chiles. It might seem strange at first, but use your finest bittersweet chocolate and you may start a new tradition in your home.

The chili can be stored, covered, in the refrigerator for up to 3 days or may be frozen for up to 3 months.

Olive oil

2 pounds bison shoulder meat (see Notes), cut into 1-inch chunks

Kosher salt and freshly ground black pepper

2 pounds ground bison (see Note)

2 large red onions, diced

6 garlic cloves, minced

6 Anaheim chiles, stemmed, seeded, and chopped (see Sources, page 233)

3 cups dried pinto beans, sorted through and soaked overnight

2 ancho chiles, stemmed, seeded, toasted, and torn into pieces (see page 41; see Sources, page 233)

1 chipotle chile (see Note, page 41)

2 tablespoons ground cumin

2 tablespoons ground coriander

1 tablespoon hot pimenton (see Note, page 65)

One 28- to 29-ounce can tomato puree

6 tablespoons tomato paste

One 28-ounce can whole peeled plum tomatoes with their juices (see page 8)

3 cups Dark Chicken Stock (page 208)

2 cups dark beer such as Guinness or Aventinus

Fresh or thawed corn kernels (cooked), lime wedges, tortilla chips, chopped fresh flat-leaf parsley, chopped fresh cilantro, chopped scallions, chopped jalapeño peppers, chopped red onions, grated dark chocolate

1. Preheat a 6½-quart slow cooker to Low.
2. Place a large heavy sauté pan over medium heat. Lightly coat the bottom of the pan with olive oil. Season the bison chunks with salt and pepper. Brown the bison chunks in batches. Transfer the bison chunks to the slow cooker insert. Add the ground bison and continue browning until the meat is lightly browned, about 10 minutes. Transfer the ground bison to the insert.
3. Add the onions to the sauté pan and cook until they are caramelized and soft. Add the garlic and Anaheim chiles and cook until the garlic is very fragrant and slightly softened. Be careful not to overbrown the garlic. Add the onion mixture to the insert.
4. Drain the beans and add them to the insert. Add the ancho chiles, chipotle chile, cumin, coriander, pimenton, tomato puree, tomato paste, crushed tomatoes with their juices, chicken stock, and beer. Stir to combine. Cook on Low for 6 to 8 hours, until the beans are tender.
5. Remove the chipotle chile before serving. Ladle the chili into bowls and serve hot, with your choice of garnishes.

NOTES

▶ Many kosher butchers and grocery stores now carry bison. Bison can also be found online. (See Sources, page 233.)

▶ Chipotle chiles are smoked jalapeño peppers. They can be found with a hechsher (kosher certification) online (see Sources, page 233).

▶ Pimenton is a Spanish smoked paprika. It is really not comparable to the paprika found in most grocery stores. It may be sweet or hot, and has a wonderful smokiness essential to paella, chorizo, and other Spanish delicacies. Pimenton can be found readily online or at specialty markets. (See Sources, page 233.)

Main Dishes

The only real stumbling block is fear of failure.
In cooking you've got to have a what-the-hell attitude.
—JULIA CHILD

I remember the first time I used my slow cooker—actually I remember the aroma. That morning I had thrown some browned beef and vegetables, a little wine and some herbs into the slow cooker and turned on the machine. I came home after a long day to the most welcoming bouquet of wine sauce, simmering beef, onions, and sweet garlic–infused chicken stock. It smelled like I had been there all day, slaving over dinner. I quickly boiled some water for pasta, tossed together a salad, and voilà, dinner was ready. I ate in a state of easy bliss, marveling at what this little machine could do. The best thing is that I barely broke a sweat and yet I was a hero with my family, who previously only thought of the slow cooker as the "Shabbat cooker."

It is important to remember that in the case of slow cooking, your results are only as good as the raw ingredients you put in. I am a very picky chef, and not just any dish will do for my family. I want only the best for them and never tolerate inferior ingredients or poor-quality results. Dried spices should be new, not stale, and fresh herbs should be added at the end of cooking to maximize the benefit of their flavors and fragrances. I frequently dip into my collection of dried mushrooms, my best herbs and spices, and only the most assertive wines for my slow cooker feasts. Meat (I prefer tougher cuts of meat for their deep flavor—and they have the added benefit of being inexpensive) as well as poultry should be browned before going into the pot to achieve the richest possible flavor. I like to brown my meat and vegetables the night before and store them in covered bowls in the refrigerator so they are ready to go. Before I leave for work the next day, I layer my ingredients in the slow cooker insert, set my timer, and go to work, knowing that dinner is a work-in-progress.

With some clever planning, shopping, and prepping of ingredients, you can completely change any dish's character. I like to buy whole spices and grind them right before use, so they are at their freshest peak. Grinding my own spices allows me to thrill my family one night with an exotic Curried Chicken (page 116) served with a voluptuous coconut sauce, and a Moroccan Chicken with Cracked Green Olives and Preserved Lemons (page 108) the next. Sure, you can get dinner on the table by tossing raw meat, some prepared spice packets, and water

into your slow cooker. But you will not achieve the rich, luxurious flavor—like my Veal Ragout (page 102)—that only great ingredients can provide. Most people—including me—use a slow cooker to save time and effort, but that also means allowing you a little extra time and effort to do simple things like grinding spices fresh. If you don't, the food will still be good, but a little extra effort will result in a noticeable difference.

I cannot imagine what my family's Shabbat lunches would be like without the slow cooker. Sabbath-observant Jews cannot cook a meal on Shabbat. Meals can be kept warm, but all food must be fully cooked before sundown the previous day. While I enjoy cold or room-temperature soups, tarts, and creative salads during the warmer months, there is something really wonderful about being greeted by tender, moist Falling-off-the-Bone Short Ribs (page 88) and other hearty dishes during the colder months. The slow cooker allows you to prep your meats and vegetables before the Sabbath and enjoy the fruits of your labor the next day.

My Friday afternoons during the winter months are fairly simple. I begin preparations for Shabbat dinner, and as I reach a resting point I start to "put up my cholent" (see Hamin—The Essence of Jewish Cooking, page 71) or Boiled Beef with Vegetables (page 66). I add spices, dried fruit, or mushrooms and put the cooker into its assigned spot as I carry on with Shabbat dinner preparations. I have it down to such a science that I hardly need to think about it.

Whether you are cooking for Shabbat or any meal, use the best ingredients possible and spend a little time prepping them to enjoy amazing meals with minimal effort.

Meat Entrées

The rich, concentrated flavor that results from a long, slow cooking session of tough cuts of meat would not normally be possible without the use of a slow cooker on a weeknight. I love the tough cuts. They get their intense flavor from their bones and from densely packed muscle. These cuts require liquid and slow cooking to release their stellar flavors and succulent texture. Put away your steaks and save those for quick cooking sessions on a grill or in a sauté pan. The slow cooker works best with chuck, shoulder, and shanks. These pieces of meat require a bit of planning ahead. Each dish benefits enormously from browning the meat first (see page 6) and adding aromatic vegetables, a flavorful liquid, and some seasonings. With a little planning, a well-stocked pantry, and some tender loving care, you can enjoy a memorable, complex-flavored dish every night of the week.

RUBBED BRISKET

MEAT

MAKES 10 SERVINGS

Brisket is so traditional—how can you improve upon it? My friend Julia makes brisket rubbed with spices, wrapped in foil, and slowly cooked in the oven. She swears that the spice-infused meat stays plump and juicy and keeps its hearty texture. Inspired by her technique, I decided to adapt her method for the slow cooker.

Boy, was she right! The fat melts into the meat and drips off. The bed of vegetables keeps the meat from sitting in the fat, and the flavors of the rub penetrate the meat and give it a pungent, lip-smacking flavor. To really put this over the top, I cut the cooked brisket into large chunks, toss it with my Root Beer BBQ Sauce (page 184), pile it on crusty rolls, and top it with Creamy Coleslaw (page 149). So messy and so good.

The brisket can be made 3 days ahead of serving and stored, covered, in the refrigerator, or frozen for up to 1 month. To reheat gently, preheat the oven to 300°F. Place the brisket and strained drippings or barbecue sauce in a casserole and cover. Reheat in the oven for 15 to 20 minutes.

2 tablespoons dry mustard

2 tablespoons dried thyme

2 tablespoons Ancho Chile Powder (page 200, or see Sources, page 233)

1 tablespoon ground coriander

1 tablespoon pimenton (see Note), preferably hot

1 teaspoon ground cumin

2 teaspoons ground anise seed

1 tablespoon ground ginger

¼ cup light brown sugar

One 5-pound first-cut brisket

Kosher salt and freshly ground black pepper

Olive oil

2 large Spanish onions, diced

3 medium carrots, peeled and diced

3 celery stalks, diced

1 head of garlic, unpeeled, cut in half horizontally

SUGGESTED GARNISHES

Root Beer BBQ Sauce (page 184)

1. Preheat a 6½-quart slow cooker to Low. Combine the dry mustard, thyme, ancho chile powder, coriander, pimenton, cumin, anise, ginger, and brown sugar in a small bowl.

2. Salt and pepper the brisket on both sides. Rub the brisket with a little olive oil. Generously coat the brisket on both sides with the rub.

3. Place the onions, carrots, celery, and garlic in the slow cooker insert. Lay the brisket, fat side up, on top of the vegetables. Cover and cook on Low for 8 hours.

4. Transfer the brisket to a cutting board or platter, cover loosely, and let it cool completely before slicing.

5. Strain the drippings through a fine-mesh strainer into a storage container. Discard the vegetables. Cover and refrigerate until the fat rises to the top and hardens. Remove and discard the fat. The broth can be served, heated, as a sauce with the sliced brisket. Serve with Root Beer BBQ Sauce, if you like.

NOTE

▶ Pimenton is a Spanish smoked paprika. It is really not comparable to the paprika found in most grocery stores. It may be sweet or hot, and has a wonderful smokiness essential to paella, chorizo, and other Spanish delicacies. Pimenton can be found readily online or at specialty markets. (See Sources, page 233.)

BOILED BEEF
WITH VEGETABLES

MEAT

MAKES 12 GENEROUS SERVINGS

*Everything about this classic French dish—
including the French name,* pot au feu, *which
translates to "pot on the fire"—is warm and
cozy. Friends and family have spent many
Shabbat afternoons gathered around a platter
of pot au feu accompanied by bowls of garlicky
aïoli and dishes of salt and pepper. Everyone
loves this dish. The simple, flavorful beef is cus-
tomized by each diner with whatever suits his
or her fancy. The meat practically melts in your
mouth. What a great way to pass a wintry or
rainy day!*

Olive oil

1½ pounds chuck roast, tied with a string

2 pounds brisket, trimmed of fat and tied
with string

3 pounds short ribs, trimmed of fat and
tied with string

1 head of garlic, cut in half horizontally

2 large Spanish onions, peeled, cut into
eighths with root end intact to hold
them together

8 veal marrow bones

4 medium red-skinned potatoes, cut into
large pieces

2 medium turnips, peeled and cut into
large pieces

2 medium parsnips, peeled and cut into
large pieces

4 large carrots, peeled and cut into large
pieces

Bouquet garni of 6 thyme sprigs, 6 flat-
leaf parsley sprigs, and 2 bay leaves,
tied together with kitchen twine

SUGGESTED ACCOMPANIMENTS
Homemade Aïoli (page 185) or Herbed Aïoli
Dipping Sauce (page 186), Parsley Sauce
(page 180), fleur de sel or other coarse sea
salt, cracked peppercorns, Dijon mustard,
baguettes cut into thick rounds and toasted
(optional), cornichons

1. Preheat a 6½-quart slow cooker to Low. Place a large sauté pan over medium heat. Lightly coat the bottom of the pan with olive oil. Brown the meats, in batches, until they are deeply caramelized. Transfer the meats to the slow cooker insert. Pour out all the fat from the pan.

2. Add ¼ to ½ cup of water to the sauté pan and scrape up all the browned bits (*sucs*; see page 7). Add this to the insert.

3. Place the garlic, onions, bones, potatoes, turnips, parsnips, and carrots on top of the meats in the insert. Bury the bouquet garni in the vegetables. Add water up to about one-half the depth of the vegetables. Cover and cook on Low for 16 hours.

4. Remove the meats and cut them into large chunks. Arrange them on a serving platter with the vegetables and bones. Skim the fat off the broth (see page 100). Pour the broth into a heatproof pitcher to pass at the table along with the accompaniments. Serve hot or at room temperature.

GARLICKY POT ROAST

MAKES 6 TO 8 SERVINGS

Something magical seems to happen when this dish cooks for a long time— the meat becomes fragrant and the garlic becomes caramelized and sweet. The "gravy" that results is so delicious that I often find one of my kids hanging around the kitchen with bread in hand to sop it up. The addition of the gingersnaps to the dish might seem odd, but they add a lot of flavor and help thicken the gravy.

The roast can be stored, covered, in the refrigerator for 3 days, or frozen for 1 month. To reheat the pot roast, place the meat and gravy in a saucepan. Add enough chicken stock to moisten the meat, usually only about ¼ cup. Cover and cook on low heat until heated through.

FOR THE MARINADE

3 tablespoons chopped garlic
(about 4 large cloves)

¼ cup light brown sugar

¼ cup olive oil, plus extra for browning
the roast

½ cup balsamic vinegar

2 tablespoons tomato paste

Kosher salt and freshly ground black
pepper

One 3- to 5-pound chuck roast, fat
trimmed

Olive oil

FOR THE SAUCE

2 large Spanish onions, chopped

6 garlic cloves, chopped

1 cup dark beer such as Guinness or
Aventinus

1 whole head of Roasted Garlic (page
212)

2 cups Essential Chicken Stock (page 207)

1 cup crumbled gingersnaps (about 15
small cookies; store-bought are fine)

¼ cup tomato paste

1. **Marinate the Roast.** In a bowl large enough to hold the roast, stir together the chopped garlic, brown sugar, olive oil, vinegar, tomato paste, and 1 tablespoon each salt and pepper. Add the roast and turn it to coat on all sides. Cover the bowl and marinate for at least 3 hours, or overnight in the refrigerator.

2. Place a large sauté pan over medium heat. Lightly coat the bottom of the pan with olive oil. Remove the roast from the marinade and pat dry. Discard the marinade. Lightly season the roast with salt and pepper. Brown the meat on all sides, about 7 minutes per side. Set aside the roast but do not clean the pan.

3. Preheat a 6½-quart slow cooker to High.

4. **Make the Sauce.** Add the onions to the sauté pan and cook until brown, 3 to 5 minutes. Add the chopped garlic and cook for 2 to 3 minutes more, until the garlic is very fragrant and has softened slightly; do not let the garlic brown. Add the beer. Scrape up the browned bits (*sucs*; see page 7) with a wooden spoon or spatula. Transfer the mixture to the slow cooker insert.

5. Place the roast and any collected juices in the insert. Squeeze the roasted garlic out of the skin and into the insert. Add the stock, gingersnaps, and tomato paste. Stir together. Cover and cook the roast on High for 7 to 8 hours, until it can be pierced easily with a fork.

6. Remove the roast from the cooker and keep warm. Strain the sauce before serving. Cut the roast into large chunks and serve hot with your choice of accompaniment. Pass the sauce.

BROWN SUGAR–GLAZED
CORNED BEEF

MAKES 8 TO 10 SERVINGS

This sweet and slightly spicy brisket is a welcome treat for lunch or a casual dinner. I often make this brisket for Passover dinner. Leave out the mustard powder during Passover. The flavor will still be delicious.

1 cup dark brown sugar

½ teaspoon ground cloves

¼ teaspoon freshly grated nutmeg

1 tablespoon freshly cracked black peppercorns

¼ cup honey

2 tablespoons dry mustard

1 tablespoon ground ginger

2 teaspoons cayenne pepper, or more (optional)

3 medium Spanish onions, roughly chopped

1 whole head garlic, cut in half horizontally

2 celery stalks, chopped

2 medium carrots, peeled and chopped

5 pounds small new potatoes, unpeeled

2 heads sturdy cabbage such as savoy, cut into wedges about 2 inches thick

Kosher salt and freshly ground black pepper

One 7-pound first-cut pickled brisket, trimmed of visible fat and cut in half to fit in the slow cooker

① Preheat a 6½-quart slow cooker to Low.

② To make the glaze, mix the brown sugar, cloves, nutmeg, peppercorns honey, mustard, ginger, and cayenne in a small bowl.

③ Place the onions, garlic, celery, carrots, potatoes, and cabbage in the bottom of the slow cooker insert. Season the vegetables lightly with salt and pepper.

④ Place the brisket pieces on top of the vegetables. It is okay if the pieces of brisket overlap in the slow cooker. Pack the glaze mixture on top of the brisket. Use all of it.

⑤ Cover and cook on Low for 8 hours, until the brisket is very tender.

⑥ Remove the brisket and set aside to cool. Remove the vegetables. Separate the potatoes and cabbage and place them back into the insert to keep warm. Discard the remaining vegetables.

⑦ Allow the brisket to cool slightly before slicing. Slice the meat thinly across the grain. Serve warm or at room temperature, with the potatoes and cabbage.

HAMIN—THE ESSENCE OF JEWISH COOKING

I was once asked for an example of a classic "Jewish dish." After some hesitation, I decided on *hamin* (ha-MEEN), the Sabbath stew. Our ancestors had to find creative ways to serve a hot meal on a day that forbids work and cooking fires—long before the invention of the slow cooker. Religious tradition and practice fostered the birth of this dish—for which you begin the cooking process before the Sabbath starts at sundown, then let it finish cooking in the oven overnight—which has been adapted around the world. Hamin, dafina, cholent, haminado, and more are different names for the same dish.

Hamin, a dish still eaten by Sephardic Jews around the world, is derived from the Hebrew word *ham*, which means "hot." Hamin's Eastern European cousin cholent (or *shalet*) is probably similarly derived from the French words *chaud* or "hot" and *lent* meaning "slow." Dafina (page 77) is the Moroccan version. In Yemen, *yaris* is the Sabbath dish and in Spain, *huevos haminados* (Roasted or Stewed Eggs, page 156) are eggs served by themselves or in a stew called *haminado*, which means "warmed."

The names and ingredients vary, but the basic concept for this Sabbath stew is the same all over the world. Ashkenazi Jews use beef, chicken, goose, legumes, and grains. Sephardic Jews use beef, mutton or lamb, chicken, legumes, and grains. The addition of a dumpling is also universal. The dumpling adds flavor and also helps to "stretch" the meal (it is said that on Shabbat, Jews are endowed with *neshama yetera*, or an extra soul that needs feeding as well). The cooking

HAMIN *continued*

technique is also universal. Aromatic vegetables like onions and garlic are browned along with the meat. Legumes and grains are added. The ingredients are then covered and placed in a very low-temperature oven until the next day when the dish is typically served after the return from synagogue.

The addition of eggs in hamin is supposed to symbolize the unremitting mourning for the destruction of the temple. Mourning aside, the eggs are a delicious and universal addition. The eggs are added raw, in the shell, to the hamin. The long slow cooking process allows the eggs to take on the flavors of the onions, spices, and meat. Outside and in, they become a beautiful coffee color (much like *huevos haminados* [Roasted or Stewed Eggs], page 156), and the inside is smooth and silky.

The importance of eating this Sabbath meal cannot be understated. The belief that the Oneg Shabbat, or enjoyment of the Sabbath, should be honored not only by wearing one's finest clothes, purchasing and preparing the finest foods that one can afford, but also by eating a hot meal on a day that forbids the lighting of fires, is a paradox. Preparation for the Sabbath meal was frequently started in the home and then continued in a public oven or often at a bakery. I talked with several Moroccan friends who remembered their mothers or sisters taking the hamin pot to the local communal oven and entrusting an Arab worker (who was not subject to kosher restrictions on cooking) to remember which pot belonged to which household. The hamin would cook overnight and the family would pick up the pot on the way home from the synagogue. I have heard similar stories from people from Poland, France, and other countries, where they took their pots to Christian bakeries whose fires were lit around the clock. It was so important to have this dish, it was entrusted to someone else to tend the fire. My friend Avi, part-time *mashgiach* (kashrut supervisor) and full-time food lover, told me that his mother would seal her pot with dough and make a mark in the dough that identified her hamin from that of her neighbors.

While hamin is considered an "old-fashioned" food, it is enjoying a resurgence in popularity. My friend Edie plans her annual Cholent Fest weeks and sometimes months in advance. Edie makes an amazing cholent and invites numerous friends over who gather around the table for an afternoon of eating and talking. Each time I enjoy her one-pot wonder, it is slightly different. Sometimes Kishke (page 75), a sausage or pudding made from matzah meal or flour, onions, and spices stuffed into a casing, is the added ingredient. Other times it is beef sausages or hot dogs. I remember a debate one year about adding beer to the mix. Regardless, it is always delicious, heartwarming, and familiar.

Recipes for Dafina (page 77) differ from region to region, according to several friends from different parts of Morocco. One described his family's recipe as a "religion unto itself." Still, Moroccans are united in their passion for the dish. One thing that is common across all versions is the addition of raw eggs in their shells before cooking.

I know many vegetarians who take their hamin quite seriously. Lack of meat does not diminish the dish. Dried mushrooms, multiple grains, roasted vegetables, and seitan are in the vegetarian's arsenal of ingredients for the Sabbath meal. The variety of adaptations is endless.

It is hard to accurately describe the flavor of a hamin to someone who has never experienced a dish that had been cooked for so many hours (frequently more than 20 hours) with so many ingredients. At a loss for words, I frequently tell initiates that hamin tastes like itself. The dish is soulful and reflects the very essence of Judaism. Preparation of this essential dish is no longer a vexing problem. With careful planning and a little kitchen prep the slow cooker takes over the task.

CHOLENT

MEAT

MAKES 8 SERVINGS

Cholent—a hearty beef and potato stew—feels as familiar and easy to me as my favorite reading chair. While there are infinite ways to flavor this Eastern European classic, I tend to save my more exotic spices and ingredients for other dishes. Some traditions, like this dish, are better left intact, although the modern touch of using the slow cooker makes it much easier to keep the tradition alive. A big pot of cholent is the perfect companion on a long Saturday afternoon with family and friends.

Olive oil

Kosher salt and freshly ground black pepper

3 pounds chuck roast or brisket, cut into 3-inch chunks

3 large Spanish onions, cut into large wedges

3 garlic cloves, chopped

2 cups dark beer such as Guinness or Aventinus

1 tablespoon tomato paste

2 cups dried kidney beans, sorted through, soaked overnight, and drained

1 cup pearled barley

4 large Yukon gold potatoes, peeled and sliced about 1½ inches thick

2 teaspoons kosher salt

1 teaspoon freshly ground black pepper

8 large eggs in their shells

1 recipe Kishke (recipe follows), cooked

1. Preheat a 6½-quart slow cooker to Low.

2. Place a large sauté pan over medium-high heat. Lightly coat the bottom of the pan with olive oil.

3. Salt and pepper the meat on all sides. Place the meat in the heated pan and brown on all sides, in batches if necessary. Transfer the meat to the slow cooker insert.

4. Add the onions to the pan. Cook the onions until they are browned and slightly softened. Add the garlic and cook until the garlic is very fragrant and has softened slightly. Transfer the onions and garlic to the insert.

5. Add the beer to the sauté pan. Scrape up any browned bits (*sucs*; see page 7) with a spatula. Add the tomato paste and stir to combine. Transfer the liquid to the insert.

6. Add the kidney beans, barley, potatoes, salt, and pepper to the slow cooker. Stir with a

large spoon to combine. Gently bury the eggs in the mixture. Cover and cook on Low for at least 10 hours.

7. About 3 hours before serving, place the whole unwrapped cooked kishke on top of the cholent. Cover and cook until you are ready to eat.

8. While many families serve the cholent right out of the slow cooker, I like to spread out the ingredients a bit. I recommend using a slotted spoon and scooping the kishke onto a platter. Then scoop some the cholent onto another platter or into a large bowl. Finally, peel the eggs from their shells, slice them into wedges, and add the wedges to the kishke platter.

KISHKE

MAKES 12 SERVINGS

I was never a big fan of kishke until I started making my own. This savory homemade dumpling simply has more flavor than the store-bought version. Traditionally, kishke is held together with schmaltz (chicken fat). Today, many cooks substitute vegetable oil for the animal fat to have a pareve version, but I prefer working with a flavorful twist on the original: duck fat! Kishke can be also be served as a side dish with Kasha Varnishkes (page 154).

2 celery stalks

2 medium carrots, peeled

1 large Spanish onion

½ cup duck fat, melted and cooled, or canola oil

1½ cups all-purpose flour

1 teaspoon sweet paprika

2 teaspoons kosher salt

1 teaspoon freshly ground black pepper

continues

1. Grate the celery, carrots, and onion in a food processor fitted with a grating blade or by hand on the coarse side of a box grater.

2. Mix the celery, carrots, onion, fat, flour, paprika, salt, and pepper in a large bowl by hand or in a mixer until the mixture forms a ball and clings together.

3. Place a large sheet of parchment paper on a work surface. Roll the dough on the parchment into a log shape about 1½ inches thick and 12 inches long. Roll the parchment paper around the log.

4. Wrap the parchment-wrapped kishke log with several layers of plastic wrap to form a waterproof package.

5. Place a large saucepan filled with several inches of water over medium heat. Bring the water to a simmer. Poach the kishke in the water for 1 hour until the kishke feels firm and solid.

6. Carefully remove the kishke and allow it to cool completely before unwrapping or slicing. Kishke may be made up to 3 days before serving and stored, covered, in the refrigerator. It may also be frozen for up to 3 months. Reheat kishke in a covered casserole in the oven at 350°F.

DAFINA

Dafina is the Moroccan equivalent of Cholent (page 74). This dish is meant to be eaten on Shabbat afternoon, served hot. The name means "covered" and refers to either the cooking vessel it is prepared in or the technique of burying an accompanying wheat-based dish in the stew while it cooks. I have included two variations for authentic Moroccan dafina. Some families use an accompanying side dish of toasted wheat berries and others swear by a hearty, fragrant rice dumpling called kouclas bi ruz. *After many trials and tastings, it is unanimous in my house: We love both, for different reasons. I suggest you experiment in your own home and see which version wins over the crowd. Both are delicious.*

My friend Marc Botbol says his family passes ground toasted cumin to sprinkle on top of the dafina.

FOR THE DAFINA

1 pound veal marrow bones (optional)
Olive oil
1 large Spanish onion, thinly sliced

1 teaspoon saffron threads
4 garlic cloves, chopped
3 pounds brisket or chuck roast, cut into
　3 × 5–inch chunks
Kosher salt and freshly gound black
　pepper
2 cups dried chick peas, sorted through,
　soaked overnight, and drained
12 small new potatoes, peeled
3 tablespoons Moroccan Spice Mix (page
　201)
8 pitted dates
8 large eggs in their shells
2 cups Essential Chicken Stock (page 207)

FOR THE WHEAT BERRIES

Olive oil
1 large Spanish onion, peeled and
　chopped
2 garlic cloves, finely chopped
1 cup basmati rice, rinsed
½ cup wheat berries, rinsed
3 cups Essential Chicken Stock (page 207)

continues

FOR THE *KOUCLAS BI RUZ* (MOROCCAN RICE DUMPLING)

½ pound ground beef or lamb
¾ cup ground walnuts or unblanched
   almonds
¼ cup sugar
½ cup chopped fresh flat-leaf parsley
2 large eggs, whisked lightly
1 cup uncooked basmati rice, preferably
   brown basmati
1 tablespoon Moroccan Spice Mix (page
   201)
1 teaspoon kosher salt
Freshly ground black pepper

SUGGESTED GARNISHES
Ground toasted cumin (optional)

1. **Make the Dafina.** If using the marrow bones, preheat the oven to 400°F. Rub the bones with olive oil and place them in a roasting pan. Roast the bones for 45 minutes until they are very dark brown but not black. Transfer the bones to the slow cooker insert.

2. Preheat a 6½-quart slow cooker to Low.

3. Place a large sauté pan over medium heat. Lightly coat the bottom of the pan with olive oil.

4. Add the onion and saffron and cook, stirring occasionally, until the onion is brown and very soft, about 15 minutes. Add the garlic and cook for several minutes until the garlic is very fragrant and has softened slightly. Transfer the onion and garlic to the slow cooker insert.

5. Season the meat with salt and pepper. Add a little more oil to the sauté pan and brown the meat in batches on all sides, 5 to 7 minutes. Transfer the meat to the insert. Add the chick peas, potatoes, spice mix, and dates to the insert. Stir with a large spoon to combine. Gently bury the eggs in the mixture.

6. **Make the Wheat Berries.** Place a clean sauté pan over medium heat. Lightly coat the bottom of the pan with olive oil. Add the onion and sauté until the onion is translucent and softened. Add the garlic, rice, and wheat berries. Continue cooking until the rice has turned a golden brown, 3 to 5 minutes.

7. My friend Isaac Elkayam says to enclose the wheat mixture in a piece of foil that has been poked with small holes. Bury the foil into the dafina with the top of the foil packet still exposed. Or, like Coty Finegold, place the wheat mixture in an earthenware cup and bury the cup only enough so you can pull it out.

8. Add the chicken stock to the dafina mixture. Add water to barely cover.

9. **Make the *Kouclas*.** Mix the ground meat, ground nuts, sugar, parsley, whisked eggs, rice, spice mix, salt, and pepper together in a large bowl. Knead the mixture to get a smooth texture.

10. Cut a large piece of cheesecloth. Place the mixture in the cheesecloth. Roll the mixture into a sausage shape about 1½ × 10 inches. Tie the ends with kitchen twine. Place the dumpling on top of the dafina.

11. Cover and cook on Low for 15 hours.

12. **Serve the Dafina.** Carefully remove the *kouclas*. Unwrap it, cut into chunks, and place it on a platter. Remove the wheat mixture and place it in a serving bowl or on the platter next to the *kouclas*. Remove the eggs and place them in a separate bowl or on the platter. Spoon the dafina into another bowl or onto the platter. Place the marrow bones, if using, in another bowl or on the platter. Each person can customize her or his own plate. Pass the ground cumin, if using.

VARIATION

Marc Botbol and his family make the wheat berries separately as he learned the technique from his mother who is from Casablanca and always made it that way.

Olive oil
1 small Spanish onion, diced
1 garlic clove, diced
1 cup wheat berries, rinsed
3 cups Essential Chicken Stock (page 207)
    or water
Kosher salt and freshly ground black
    pepper

1. Preheat the oven to 200°F.
2. Place a small sauté pan over medium heat. Lightly coat the bottom of the pan with olive oil. Sauté the onion until it is lightly browned and softened, about 10 minutes. Add the garlic and continue cooking until the garlic is very fragrant and has softened slightly, about 2 minutes.
3. Transfer the onion mixture to a medium ovenproof casserole. Stir in the wheat berries and chicken stock. Season with salt and pepper. Cover and cook overnight, until the wheat berries are soft but still chewy.

CASSEROLE OF BEEF AND PEPPERS

MEAT

MAKES 8 SERVINGS

At its heart, this simple casserole dish—also called carne guisada—*lets the meat, onions, and peppers speak for themselves. I like to serve it with my favorite chewy short-grain brown rice or sometimes we like to roll it up in toasted tortillas and serve with a squeeze of lime juice.*

I have been eating different variations of this dish for more than a decade. It is the kind of meal that one of my staff members would cook slowly all day until it was time for our restaurant staff meal, also called the family meal. The dish varied depending upon the cook, where in Mexico he grew up, which family he comes from (I have employed many sets of brothers in my restaurants), and, of course, personal preferences.

3 pounds beef chuck, cut into 2-inch chunks

Kosher salt and freshly ground black pepper

Olive oil

3 large Spanish onions, thinly sliced

2 red bell peppers, stemmed, seeded, and cut into thin strips

1 green bell pepper, stemmed, seeded, and cut into thin strips

2 jalapeño peppers, stemmed, seeded, and cut into thin strips (optional)

6 garlic cloves, thinly sliced

2 cups Essential Chicken Stock (page 207)

3 fresh large plum tomatoes, seeded and chopped, or 1 cup drained canned whole peeled plum tomatoes, crushed (see page 8)

Chef Laura's Famous Guacamole (page 20), chopped cilantro, chopped red onion, fresh lime juice, diced jalapeño peppers

SUGGESTED ACCOMPANIMENTS
Steamed white rice, roasted potatoes, sautéed hearty greens such as Swiss chard, warm tortillas

1. Preheat a slow cooker to Low.
Season the meat with salt and pepper. Place a large sauté pan over medium-high heat. Lightly coat the bottom of the pan with olive oil. Brown the meat, in batches, on all sides, 5 to 7 minutes, until the pieces are caramelized and have a browned crust. Transfer the meat to the slow cooker insert.

2. Add the onions and peppers into the same pan while it is still hot. Add more oil if necessary. Cook the vegetables over medium-low heat, stirring occasionally, until the onions are very soft and lightly browned, about 30 minutes. Add the garlic at the end and cook for 3 minutes more.

3. Transfer the vegetables to the slow cooker insert. Add the remaining ingredients. Cover and cook on Low for 6 hours or until the meat is very tender.

4. Adjust the seasoning with salt and pepper. Ladle the fragrant beef and its juices over your choice of accompaniments, or scoop up the meat into tortillas and garnish as desired.

BRACIOLE

MEAT

MAKES 6 SERVINGS

Braciole are thin slices of meat, poultry, fish, or vegetables wrapped around a filling and typically cooked in a wine sauce. Sometimes referred to as involtini, *this Sicilian dish has many variations (see Halibut Involtini, page 126). Many of the steps can be done ahead of time, so the dish is a delicious option for Shabbat dinner. I like to serve it with Toasted Capellini (page 144).*

The filling can be made up to 3 days before using. Store the filling, covered, in the refrigerator, or freeze for up to 1 month. The braciole can be made 3 days ahead of serving and stored in its sauce, covered, in the refrigerator, or frozen for up to 1 month. To reheat gently, preheat the oven to 300°F. Place the braciole and its sauce in a casserole and cover. Reheat in the oven for 15 to 20 minutes.

FOR THE FILLING

Olive oil

1 large Spanish onion, very thinly sliced

1 whole head of Roasted Garlic (page 212)

3 tightly packed cups baby spinach

One 28-ounce can whole peeled plum tomatoes, drained (juice reserved) and crushed (see page 8)

3 tablespoons chopped fresh thyme leaves

3 tablespoons chopped fresh flat-leaf parsley

¼ cup toasted pine nuts (see page 199)

½ cup golden raisins

Pinch of chili flakes (optional)

3 tablespoons tomato paste

¼ cup fresh bread crumbs (leftover challah works well)

Kosher salt and freshly ground black pepper

FOR THE SAUCE

2 cups dry red wine such as Chianti

Reserved juices from canned tomatoes

2 tablespoons tomato paste

2 cups Dark Chicken Stock (page 208) or Veal Stock (page 210)

2 medium carrots, peeled and chopped

1 celery stalk, chopped

1 medium red onion, chopped

Several thyme sprigs

2 garlic cloves, peeled and lightly crushed

One 4- to 5-pound top chuck roast, butterflied to open up to approximately 13 × 9 inches (ask your butcher to butterfly it or see below)

SUGGESTED ACCOMPANIMENTS
Toasted Capellini (page 144), potatoes

1. **Make the Filling.** Place a medium saucepan over medium-low heat. Lightly coat the bottom of the pan with oil. Slowly cook the onion, stirring occasionally, until it is very soft and lightly browned, about 10 minutes.

2. Squeeze the roasted garlic out of the skin and mix it with the onion. Add the spinach, tomatoes, thyme, parsley, pine nuts, raisins, chili flakes (if using), tomato paste, bread crumbs, and salt and pepper. Increase the heat to medium. Cook until the mixture is very thick, about 15 minutes. Transfer the filling to a bowl and cool completely.

3. **Make the Sauce.** Place the wine in a large saucepan over medium-high heat and simmer until the wine is reduced by half, about 15 minutes. Transfer the wine to the insert of a 6½-quart slow cooker. Add the reserved tomato juices, tomato paste, stock, carrots, celery, onion, thyme, and crushed garlic to the insert. Preheat a slow cooker to Low.

4. Open up the butterflied meat. Pound the meat with a mallet until it is a uniform thickness, 1 to 1½ inches. Salt and pepper the inside of the meat. Spread the filling evenly over the meat, leaving a 1½-inch border at the top. Roll the meat from the long edge, jelly-roll style. Tie knots fairly snugly every 2 inches to secure the meat and filling.

5. Place a large sauté pan over medium-high heat. Lightly coat the bottom of the pan with olive oil. Brown the meat on all sides. Transfer the meat to the insert. Cover and cook on Low for 6 hours until the meat is very tender.

6. Gently remove the meat with a slotted spoon or spatula and transfer to a platter or cutting board. Cut the meat into 2-inch slices and serve with Toasted Capellini or potatoes. Pass extra sauce.

- -

HOW TO BUTTERFLY MEAT OR FISH

If you are right-handed, place the thick end of your chuck roast toward your right; reverse if you are left-handed. Using a sharp chef's knife, cut through the thick end toward the thinner end, keeping your knife parallel to the cutting board. I use short strokes and keep my other hand flat on top of the meat. When you reach about one inch from the end, stop cutting and simply pound out the end piece (now the middle) with a meat mallet.

- -

BELGIAN SWEET-AND-SOUR
BEEF AND ONION STEW

MAKES 6 SERVINGS

I have to credit the Belgian ale in this stew—called carbonnade flamande *in Belgium—for doing a great deal of the work. The ale adds a sweet, earthy, and somewhat sour flavor that permeates the entire dish. The bread will slowly dissolve into the braising liquid to thicken it and make the sauce creamy and rich.*

The carbonnade can be made 3 days ahead of serving and stored, covered, in the refrigerator, or frozen for up to 1 month. To reheat gently, preheat the oven to 300°F. Place the beef and its sauce in a casserole and cover.

3 pounds beef shoulder or chuck, cut into 2-inch cubes
Kosher salt and freshly ground black pepper
½ cup all-purpose flour
Olive oil
3 large Spanish onions, thinly sliced
6 garlic cloves, chopped
½ cup Essential Chicken Stock (page 207)
½ cup Veal Stock (page 210)

One 11-ounce bottle Chimay or favorite Belgian ale
Bouquet garni of 6 thyme sprigs, 1 bay leaf, and 6 parsley sprigs, tied together with kitchen twine
¼ cup dark brown sugar
2 tablespoons Dijon mustard
1 thick slice of whole-wheat bread, toasted

SUGGESTED ACCOMPANIMENTS
Parsleyed egg noodles, steamed or boiled potatoes

1 Preheat a 6½-quart slow cooker to Low. Pat the beef dry with paper towels and season with salt and pepper. Lightly dredge the beef in the flour.

2 Place a large sauté pan over medium heat. Lightly coat the bottom of the pan with olive oil. Brown the beef cubes on all sides in batches. Transfer each batch to the slow cooker insert.

3. Add a little more oil to the sauté pan. Turn down the heat to low and cook the onions until they are very soft and quite brown, about 15 minutes. Add the garlic and cook for 5 minutes more. Transfer the onions to the insert. Return the pan to the heat.

4. Increase the heat to medium-high. Add the chicken and veal stocks to the pan. Bring to a simmer and cook for 5 minutes. Scrape up any browned bits (*sucs*; see page 7) with a wooden spoon. Transfer the liquid to the insert.

5. Add the beer, bouquet garni, and brown sugar to the insert. Stir to combine. Spread the mustard on the bread. Place the bread on top of the beef and onions in the insert.

6. Cover and cook on Low for 8 hours, until the beef is very tender. Ladle the beef and fragrant gravy into bowls piled high with your choice of accompaniment.

CASSOULET

MAKES 8 SERVINGS

I fondly remember an elderly couple who were regulars at my first restaurant. They didn't just eat dinner, they feasted. My staff and I marveled at how much they could put away, ordering one item at a time and sitting for hours, eating and enjoying each other's company. What chef wouldn't love that? The husband once told me, with a gleam in his eye, about the cassoulet that he'd made the first night of Sukkot (the Jewish harvest holiday) every year for decades. I always joked that someday I would show up at their house on Sukkot with a plate in hand. While I never actually joined them, one day the cassoulet chef's wife brought me her husband's precious handwritten cookbook including his recipe for the famous cassoulet. I treasure the notebook of recipes with personal notes and comments, and I am proud to share this adaptation of his cassoulet.

Cassoulet is a long-cooking southern French specialty of beans flavored with garlic, duck, sausages, and a creamy crust of mustard and bread crumbs. Cassoulet is remarkably similar to cholent. We serve it for special Shabbat lunches and lazy Sunday dinners.

1 pound dried white beans, preferably navy beans, sorted through, soaked overnight, and drained

2 quarts cold water

4 cups Veal Stock (page 210)

¼ cup tomato paste

2 whole large Spanish onions, peeled and studded with 3 whole cloves each

6 garlic cloves, chopped

1 celery stalk, chopped

1 bay leaf

6 flat-leaf parsley sprigs

3 fresh tomatoes, chopped, or one 14- to 15-ounce can whole peeled plum tomatoes with their juices, crushed (see page 8)

2 pounds chuck flanken with bones, or short ribs

Olive oil

4 whole legs Duck Confit (page 122)

1 pound raw garlic sausage or favorite sausage, sliced into 1-inch-thick slices

2 cups fresh bread crumbs

1 cup chopped fresh flat-leaf parsley

¼ cup Dijon mustard

A dash of hot sauce (optional)

Kosher salt and freshly ground black
pepper

Parsley Sauce (page 180)

1. Preheat a 6½-quart slow cooker to Low.
2. Place the beans in the slow cooker insert. Add the water, stock, and tomato paste. Place the onions, garlic, celery, bay leaf, and parsley sprigs on a large square of cheesecloth. Draw the corners together and tie with kitchen twine to make a bouquet garni. Add this to the beans in the insert. Add the tomatoes with their juices.
3. Bring a large saucepan of water to a boil. Add the flanken and cook for 5 minutes to boil off the fat. Set the meat aside and discard the water.
4. Place a sauté pan over medium heat. Lightly coat the bottom of the pan with olive oil. Cook the duck legs in the sauté pan until the skin has crisped and browned, about 10 minutes. Reserve several tablespoons of the duck fat in the pan. Transfer the duck to the insert.

5. Brown the sausage in the duck fat. Remove the sausage from the pan and set aside.
6. Add the bread crumbs to the sauté pan and toast them, stirring, until lightly browned. Transfer the bread crumbs to a medium bowl. Toss the bread crumbs with the chopped parsley and Dijon mustard until they form a moist, crumbly texture. Cover the bowl and set aside.
7. Gently push the flanken and sausage into the beans so the beans cover them. Add a dash of hot sauce (if using). Cook the cassoulet on Low for 8 hours until the beans are tender.
8. Season with salt and pepper. Sprinkle the bread crumb mixture over the top of the casserole. Cover and cook for 30 minutes more, until all the liquid has been absorbed. Serve with Parsley Sauce.

FALLING-OFF-THE-BONE SHORT RIBS

MEAT

MAKES 8 TO 10 SERVINGS

There aren't many short rib preparations that I haven't enjoyed. This versatile, tasty cut of beef gives us everything you can ask for in beef: You get marbled beef, and bones for flavor. This recipe is especially succulent. Ask your butcher for "English cut" short ribs. This cut tends to be tender, makes a better presentation, and is very economical. (The other common cut for short ribs is "flanken cut," which is great in soups and stews.)

5 pounds beef short ribs

**Kosher salt and freshly ground black
pepper**

3 tablespoons dried thyme

2 tablespoons dried rosemary

¼ cup Porcini Dust (page 202)

¼ cup all-purpose flour

Olive oil

3 celery stalks, chopped

2 large Spanish onions, chopped

3 medium carrots, peeled and chopped

**1 medium fennel bulb, trimmed, cored,
and chopped**

6 garlic cloves, chopped

**2 cups red wine such as cabernet
sauvignon**

3 tablespoons tomato paste

3 cups Essential Chicken Stock (page 207)

**Bouquet garni of 1 bay leaf, 6 thyme
sprigs, 6 parsley sprigs, and 1 small
rosemary sprig, tied together with
kitchen twine**

SUGGESTED ACCOMPANIMENTS
Simple Grits (page 146), White Bean Ragù
(page 101)

1. Place the short ribs in a large stockpot filled with water and bring to a boil. Boil the short ribs for 5 minutes. Drain and discard the water. (This helps remove the fat.)

2. Pat dry the ribs thoroughly with a paper towel. Season the ribs with salt and pepper.

3. Combine the dried thyme, dried rosemary, porcini dust, and flour in a bowl.

4. Place a large sauté pan over medium heat. Lightly coat the bottom of the pan with olive oil. Dredge the ribs in the porcini mixture. Brown the ribs in batches until the ribs are browned on all sides, about 15 minutes. Transfer the ribs to the insert of a 6½-quart slow cooker.

5 Pour off most of the fat from the sauté pan. Brown the celery, onions, carrots, and fennel in batches, about 7 minutes per batch. Season each batch with salt and pepper. Add the garlic to the last batch and cook for 3 minutes more, until the garlic is very fragrant and slightly softened. Do not over-brown the garlic.

6 Transfer the browned vegetables to the insert. Add the wine and the tomato paste to the sauté pan. Stir together with a wooden spoon or spatula to break up the tomato paste. Gently scrape the pan to gather up the browned bits (*sucs*; see page 7).

7 Transfer the wine to the insert. Add the stock and bouquet garni. Cover and cook on Low for 10 hours.

8 Remove the short ribs from the insert and place them on a platter. Tent loosely with foil to keep them warm. Pour the braising liquid through a fine-mesh strainer into a saucepan. Discard the vegetables and bouquet garni. Skim the fat off the liquid. Reduce over high heat by one half, or until the liquid is thick and coats the back of a spoon, about 10 minutes. Pour the sauce over the ribs.

9 Serve with your choice of accompaniment.

STUFFED CABBAGE ROLLS

MEAT

MAKES 6 SERVINGS

This dish, called holishkes *in Yiddish, is pure Eastern European comfort food. There are many versions of the sauce and filling depending on which region the recipe originates from. Personally, I like to use barley in the filling as it adds a nutty flavor and chewy texture. I also enjoy the subtle fragrance a cinnamon stick adds. Holishkes are often served during Sukkot (the Jewish harvest holiday) to represent hope for abundance in the New Year.*

The holishkes can be stored, covered, in the sauce, for up to 3 days in the refrigerator, or frozen for 1 month. To reheat gently, preheat the oven to 300°F. Place the cabbage rolls in a casserole, add about ¼ cup chicken stock or water, and cover. Reheat in the oven for 20 to 30 minutes.

1 large head green cabbage (about 2 pounds)

FOR THE STUFFING

⅓ cup pearled barley
1 cup Essential Chicken Stock (page 207) or water

1 small shallot, chopped
1 garlic clove, crushed
Kosher salt and freshly ground black pepper
Olive oil
2 large Spanish onions, finely chopped
3 garlic cloves, chopped
1 pound ground beef
3 tablespoons tomato paste

FOR THE SAUCE

2 tablespoons olive oil
3 garlic cloves, chopped
1 large Spanish onion, thinly sliced
One 28-ounce can whole peeled plum tomatoes, drained (juice reserved) and crushed (see page 8)
¼ cup tomato paste
2 tablespoons sugar
¼ cup cider vinegar
One 2- to 3-inch cinnamon stick
2 cups Essential Chicken Stock (page 207)
Kosher salt and freshly ground black pepper

1. Fill a stockpot large enough to hold the cabbage three-quarters full and bring to the boil. Place the cabbage into the boiling water, reduce the heat to a simmer, and cook uncovered for 10 minutes. Remove the cabbage from the pot and set aside until cool enough to handle.

2. Slice off the bottom of the cabbage at the core. Gently peel the leaves from the cabbage, taking care to not tear them. (If they tear slightly, it is fine.) Set aside.

3. **Make the Stuffing.** Place the barley, chicken stock, shallot, and crushed garlic in a small saucepan. Season with salt and pepper. Cover and cook for 30 minutes until the barley is soft but still slightly al dente.

4. Meanwhile, place a large sauté pan over medium heat. Lightly coat the bottom of the pan with olive oil. Cook the onions, stirring occasionally, until they are translucent and very limp but not browned, 7 to 10 minutes. Add the chopped garlic and cook for 3 minutes more, until the garlic is very fragrant and has softened. Increase the heat to medium-high and add the ground beef. Cook the beef, stirring occasionally, until it is no longer pink, about 10 minutes.

5. Add the tomato paste and the cooked barley. Stir to combine. Remove from the heat, season with salt and pepper, and set aside to cool.

6. **Make the Sauce.** Place the olive oil, garlic, Spanish onion, tomatoes with their juices, tomato paste, sugar, vinegar, cinnamon stick, and stock into the insert of a 6½-quart slow cooker. Stir to combine. Preheat a slow cooker to Low.

7. Trim the hard white core from the center of each cabbage leaf. Place a leaf in front of you with the bottom (stem) edge closest to you. Place 2 tablespoons of filling in the center of the leaf. Roll up the bottom edge over the filling and fold over the sides. Continue rolling up until the leaf is completely rolled into a small package. Place the leaf, seam side down, into the sauce in the slow cooker insert.

8. Continue rolling the cabbage leaves until all the filling is used, placing them into the sauce. It is okay if you have to layer the cabbage rolls. Cover and cook on Low for 5 hours.

9. The cabbage rolls should be translucent and firm to the touch. Place them on a serving dish. Adjust the seasoning of the sauce with salt and pepper. Remove the cinnamon stick. Lightly spoon the sauce over the bundles and serve piping hot.

TAMALES

MAKES 10 SERVINGS

My love for Mexican food is sometimes confusing to friends who are not familiar with the bright, complex flavors of this ancient cuisine. Mexican food varies greatly from region to region, but all authentic Mexican cuisines use fresh, in-season ingredients, unadulterated by modern substitutions. The clever use of a single ingredient in both its dried and fresh forms, as in the following recipe, wins my respect and admiration. Tamales are a labor-intensive project, but they can be prepared ahead of time. This is a true "special occasion" dish.

The masa dough can be made one day ahead of making the tamales and stored, covered, in the refrigerator. The husks can be softened one day ahead and stored in the water.

FOR THE CORN MASA

4 cups masa harina (see Notes)

1 cup corn oil

2 tablespoons chicken fat (optional)

2½ cups Essential Chicken Stock (page 207)

2 teaspoons kosher salt

FOR THE CORN HUSKS

35 dried corn husks (see Notes)

FOR THE FILLING

3 cups shredded cooked Rubbed Brisket (page 64) or cooked chicken, turkey, or other meat

1 cup Tomatillo Sauce (recipe follows)

2 tablespoons prepared masa dough

3 tablespoons chopped fresh cilantro

Kosher salt and freshly ground black pepper

SUGGESTED GARNISHES

Lime wedges, fresh cilantro leaves

SUGGESTED ACCOMPANIMENTS

Tomatillo Sauce (recipe follows), store-bought salsa, lime wedges, chopped fresh cilantro

1 **Make the Corn Masa.** Place the masa harina in the bowl of a stand mixer fitted with a paddle attachment. Add the corn oil and chicken fat, if using. Beat together for several minutes at medium speed until the mixture is well combined and the masa clings

together. Reduce the speed to low and stir in the chicken stock and salt. Increase the speed to medium and mix for 3 minutes to thoroughly combine the ingredients and produce an airy dough. Set aside the masa dough.

2 **Prepare the Corn Husks.** Separate the corn husks and remove any debris and corn silk that clings to them.

3 Place the husks in a large stockpot filled with hot water. Place a heat-resistant weight like a small saucepan on top of the corn husks. Bring the stockpot to a simmer and turn off the heat. Allow the husks to soak in the hot water until they are flexible and very soft, about 2 hours.

4 **Make the Filling.** Mix together the brisket, sauce, masa dough, cilantro, and salt and pepper in a medium bowl and set aside.

5 **Make the Tamales.** Spread a corn husk in front of you with the narrow side facing away from you. Smear 2 tablespoons of masa dough in a thick, narrow strip in the middle of the husk. Take a small handful of filling and place it in the middle of the masa dough. Fold the husk over the filling so that the dough covers the filling. The husk should close completely so that no filling comes out the side. Set aside the tamale and continue using the dough and filling until you have filled 30 of the husks.

6 Place water into the insert of a 6½-quart slow cooker to a depth of 2 inches. Place the remaining 5 corn husks in the bottom of the slow cooker. Spread them out to cover the water. Stand the filled tamales in the slow cooker and cover the slow cooker. Cook on Low for 10 hours or on High for 5 hours, until the masa is cooked through and no longer soft. The masa should feel firm but slightly spongy.

7 Serve with additional tomatillo sauce or store-bought salsa, lime wedges, and chopped cilantro. Pile the tamales on a platter with lime wedges and cilantro leaves. To eat a tamale, open up the corn husk, squeeze a bit of lime on top of the tamale, dollop with sauce, top with cilantro, and eat right from the husk.

NOTES

▶ Masa harina is a ground corn flour. It can be purchased at many grocery stores and Latin markets.
▶ Corn husks are dried and packaged in large bundles. They are easily found in many grocery stores and Latin markets.

continues

TOMATILLO SAUCE

PAREVE

MAKES 1 CUP

This quick pan sauce is an important component of tamales but it also perks up fish and poultry. By charring the tomatillos, pepper, garlic, and onion, you add a level of flavor that complements the lemony brightness of the tomatillos. If the serrano chile is too much heat for you, try a jalapeño or start with half a jalapeño, but do not eliminate the chile from the sauce. It balances the other ingredients.

I make a double batch of this sauce and freeze the extra. The sauce can be stored in the refrigerator, covered, for up to 3 days or frozen for up to 2 months.

6 medium tomatillos, husks removed, rinsed

3 large unpeeled garlic cloves

1 small Spanish onion, unpeeled

1 small whole serrano or jalapeño chile

Juice of 2 limes

½ cup extra-virgin olive oil

Kosher salt and freshly ground black pepper

1. Place the tomatillos, garlic, onion, and chile in a dry sauté pan over medium-high heat. Allow the vegetables to cook on one side until they are dark brown. Turn over and continue charring until brown on all sides.
2. Remove from the pan and allow to cool.
3. Peel the garlic and onion. Cut the chile in half and remove the stem and seeds. Try not to touch the seeds or soft inside of the pepper with your hands, or wear gloves. (The natural capsaicin in the pepper can burn your eyes if you touch them.)
4. Place the tomatillos, garlic, onion, chile, lime juice, and olive oil in a food processor or blender and process until the mixture is fairly smooth. Some chunks are okay—this is a rustic sauce. Season with salt and pepper.

SHEPHERD'S PIE

MAKES 6 SERVINGS

The unexpected surprise of spiced lamb under a bed of creamy sweet potatoes makes this dish a weeknight WOW. My version of the English classic has jazzed-up flavors and color; the dish will be one that you will crave for its simple, welcoming warmth. With a variety of vegetables and legumes, it is also nutritious.

Olive oil

1 large Spanish onion, thinly sliced

3 pounds ground lamb

2 medium carrots, peeled and cut into
    small dice

3 garlic cloves, thinly sliced

½ cup dried green split peas

½ cup dried chick peas, soaked overnight
    and drained

1½ tablespoons Curry Powder (page 198)

½ small serrano chile, stemmed, seeded,
    and diced (optional)

1 cup dark beer such as Guinness or
    Aventinus

1 cup Essential Chicken Stock (page 207)

1 tablespoon kosher salt

1 teaspoon freshly ground black pepper

3 cups Mashed Sweet Potatoes (page
    155)

1 large egg

1. Preheat a slow cooker to Low.

2. Place a large sauté pan over medium heat. Lightly coat the bottom of the pan with olive oil. Add the onion and cook, stirring occasionally, until it is very soft and browned, 10 to 15 minutes. Add the lamb and carrots and increase the heat to medium-high, continuing to cook, stirring occasionally, until the lamb is browned, about 5 minutes. Add the garlic and cook for 1 minute more. Transfer the mixture to the slow cooker insert.

3. Add the split peas, chick peas, curry powder, serrano chile (if using), beer, stock, and salt and pepper to the lamb mixture. Stir to combine. Cook on Low for 4 hours or until the chick peas are tender.

4. Preheat the oven to 400°F. If your slow cooker insert is not ovenproof, transfer the cooked meat mixture to a casserole. Spread the mashed sweet potatoes in a thick layer on top of the meat mixture in the casserole or insert. Lightly beat the egg and brush it over the top of the potatoes. Bake until the potatoes are heated through and lightly browned, about 20 minutes.

MEATLOAF

MEAT

MAKES 6 SERVINGS

This moist, tasty, hearty version of the classic dish is enough to make anyone feel good any time. The mushrooms give the meatloaf a deep, earthy flavor. This dish can be easily adapted for Passover by using matzah meal instead of bread crumbs.

The meatloaf can be made 3 days ahead of serving and can be stored, covered, in the refrigerator, or frozen for up to 1 month. To reheat gently, preheat the oven to 300°F. Place the meatloaf in a casserole, add about ¼ cup chicken stock or water, and cover. Reheat in the oven for 15 to 20 minutes. But to be honest, I like to eat leftover meatloaf right out of the refrigerator, in a sandwich.

Olive oil

1 large Spanish onion, finely chopped

2 garlic cloves, chopped

1 medium carrot, peeled and grated on the coarse side of a box grater

3 pounds ground beef chuck

¼ cup Mushroom Duxelles (page 214)

2 tablespoons chopped fresh flat-leaf parsley

1 teaspoon chopped fresh thyme leaves

2 tablespoons tomato paste

1 cup fresh bread crumbs or matzah meal (during Passover)

1 large egg, lightly whisked

Kosher salt and freshly ground black pepper

SUGGESTED ACCOMPANIMENTS

Braised Cipollini Onions in Mushroom-Peppercorn Sauce (page 182)

1. Place a medium sauté pan over medium heat. Lightly coat the bottom of the pan with olive oil. Cook the onion, stirring occasionally, until translucent and very limp. Add the garlic and cook for 3 minutes more. Place the onion and garlic in a large mixing bowl to cool completely.

2. Preheat a large oval slow cooker to Low. Line a 9 by 5-inch loaf pan with parchment paper, with 3 inches of paper hanging over each side to cover the meatloaf.

3. Add the carrot, ground beef, duxelles, parsley, thyme, tomato paste, bread crumbs, and egg to the onion and garlic. Season with salt and pepper. Gently mix everything with your hands.

4 Place the meat mixture into the loaf pan. Do not pack the mixture tightly, or the meatloaf will be tough. Cover the top of the loaf pan with the overhanging parchment paper.

5 Place the loaf pan in the slow cooker insert. Add warm water to the insert to a depth of halfway up the sides of the loaf pan. Cover and cook on Low for 5 hours, or until an instant-read thermometer registers 155°F when inserted into the center of the meatloaf.

6 Remove the meatloaf from the slow cooker. Cool the meatloaf slightly until you can comfortably touch the loaf pan. Turn the loaf pan upside down on to a platter. The meatloaf will come out easily. Remove the parchment paper. Slice and serve with Braised Cipollini Onions in Mushroom-Peppercorn Sauce.

CREAMY RISOTTO WITH ITALIAN SAUSAGE, PEPPERS, AND ONIONS

MEAT

MAKES 4 SERVINGS

This comforting rice dish has all the flavor of an Italian sausage and pepper sandwich. Risotto is normally a laborious project requiring a lot of stirring, but the slow cooker takes over much of the work. The starch in the rice releases slowly during the extended cooking process, resulting in a very creamy dish.

Olive oil

1 pound Italian sausage, cut into 1-inch pieces

2 red bell peppers, roasted (see page 37), stemmed, seeded, peeled, and cut into thin strips

1 large red onion, very thinly sliced

3 garlic cloves, chopped

4 ounces cremini mushrooms with their stems, sliced (about 1 cup)

2 cups Arborio rice

½ cup dry white wine such as pinot grigio

1 tablespoon tomato paste

4½ cups Essential Chicken Stock (page 207)

½ teaspoon chili flakes (optional)

2 tablespoons chopped fresh oregano

2 tablespoons chopped fresh flat-leaf parsley

Kosher salt and freshly ground black pepper

1. Place a large sauté pan over medium-high heat. Lightly coat the bottom of the pan with olive oil. Brown the sausage, about 5 minutes. Transfer the sausage to a slow cooker insert.

2. Add the peppers and onion to the sauté pan. Cook the onion and peppers about 10 minutes, until soft and brown. Add the garlic to the mixture and cook for 2 minutes more. Transfer the vegetables to the insert.

3. Add a small amount of oil to the sauté pan and cook the mushrooms until they are browned and slightly crispy, 5 to 7 minutes. Add the rice and stir together until the rice grains are lightly coated with the olive oil. Add the wine and simmer for 2 minutes. Stir in the tomato paste. Transfer the mushroom-rice mixture to the insert.

4. Add the chicken stock and chili flakes (if using) to the slow cooker insert. Stir together, cover, and cook on High for 2 hours until the rice is creamy but still al dente. Add the herbs and season to taste with salt and pepper.

VARIATION

Use leftover chicken or beef in place of the Italian sausage.

OSSO BUCO WITH GREMOLATA AND WHITE BEAN RAGÙ

MAKES 6 SERVINGS

Imagine a rich broth perfumed with wine, garlic, herbs, and mushrooms, and a tender piece of meat happily simmering away for hours until it is tender and full of flavor. What could be better? Osso buco is an Italian dish that means "pierced bone," probably because the dish is made from veal shank bones. After many hours of gentle simmering, the marrow from the bones becomes succulent and is often scooped out and served with toasted bread. The slow cooker makes one of my favorite dishes easy and accessible even on a weeknight. A little prep the night before and I have this gorgeous dish waiting for me after a long day.

The classic garnish of gremolata is a raw condiment of citrus zests, parsley, and garlic sprinkled over the osso buco to add a bright, sparkly flavor. In this version, I add the gremolata to the white bean ragù to provide a flavorful bed for the osso buco. (A ragù is an Italian stew or hearty sauce.) Beans usually need a long stovetop cooking session that requires tending. The slow cooker makes terrific side dishes possible. I soak my beans the night before, pop them in the slow cooker before work, and come home to a ready-to-eat meal. If you have only one slow cooker, the beans can be made up to 3 days ahead and stored, covered, in the refrigerator.

6 large, meaty 2-inch-thick slices veal shank (about 1 pound each) tied around with butcher's twine

Kosher salt and freshly ground black pepper

3 tablespoons all-purpose flour for dredging

¼ cup Herbes de Provence (page 196)

¼ cup Porcini Dust (page 202)

Olive oil

2 medium leeks, light green parts only, chopped

3 medium carrots, peeled and cut into ½-inch pieces

1 large fennel bulb, trimmed, cored, and diced (reserve the fronds for garnish)

8 garlic cloves, chopped

6 ounces cremini mushrooms with their stems, sliced (about 2 cups)

2 tablespoons tomato paste

½ cup dry white wine such as pinot grigio

1 cup Essential Chicken Stock (page 207) or Veal Stock (page 210)

White Bean Ragù (recipe follows)

SUGGESTED GARNISHES

Gremolata (page 191), reserved fennel fronds

continues

1. Preheat a 6½-quart slow cooker to Low. Sprinkle the shanks with salt and pepper. Stir together the flour, Herbes de Provence, and porcini dust in a shallow bowl. Dredge only the flat sides of the shanks in the flour mixture (do not coat the outside of the shank in flour or it may become gummy). Save any remaining flour mixture.

2. Place a large sauté pan over medium heat. Lightly coat the bottom of the pan with olive oil. Brown the shanks, in batches if necessary, on both flat sides. Transfer the shanks to the slow cooker insert.

3. Add the leeks to the sauté pan (add more oil if necessary). Cook the leeks until they are very soft and translucent, 5 to 7 minutes. Add the carrots and fennel, and cook until all the vegetables are browned, about 5 minutes. Add the garlic and cook for 2 minutes more. Transfer the vegetables to the insert.

4. Place the sauté pan back on the heat and add enough oil to lightly coat the bottom of the pan. Sauté the mushrooms until browned, about 5 minutes. Add the tomato paste and stir with the mushrooms until very fragrant, about 2 minutes, adding more oil if the paste begins to stick. Add the wine and stock. Stir together to combine. Add the mushroom mixture to the insert. Cover and cook on Low for 8 hours.

5. Use a slotted spoon to transfer the shanks to a platter. Untie the shanks and loosely tent them with foil to keep warm. If the meat falls off the bones, just plate the chunks on the setting platter with the bone. With a wire skimmer, remove the vegetables from the braising liquid and discard. Using a ladle, skim the fat off the surface of the braising liquid. (The fat will have risen to the top and can be easily skimmed off if you tip the ladle to the side and gently move along the surface of the braising liquid.) Discard the fat. If your slow cooker has an aluminum insert, place it on the stovetop and simmer the braising liquid until it has reduced by half and coats the back of a wooden spoon. Otherwise, transfer the braising liquid to a saucepan on the stovetop and simmer until it has reduced.

6. If the beans were cooked ahead of time, while the sauce is reducing reheat them in a covered casserole in the oven set at 300°F, for 15 to 20 minutes. Mound the beans on a serving platter. Place the osso buco on top of the beans and spoon sauce over the shanks. Garnish with reserved fennel fronds and additional gremolata.

WHITE BEAN RAGÙ

MAKES 6 SERVINGS

**2 cups dried cannellini beans, sorted
through and soaked overnight**

**1 whole head of Roasted Garlic (page
212)**

**4 to 5 cups Essential Chicken Stock (page
207)**

**3 tablespoons Gremolata (page 191),
made with 2 lemons and 2 oranges**

**Kosher salt and freshly ground black
pepper**

1. Place the beans in the insert of a slow cooker. Squeeze the garlic out of the skin and into the beans. Stir. Add the chicken stock. Cover the beans and cook on Low for 6 hours, until the beans are very soft.

2. Transfer the beans to a large bowl and mash them lightly. (I like to leave some of the beans chunky and whole.) Stir in the gremolata and salt and pepper to taste. Return to the slow cooker, set to Low or Warm (if the cooker has that setting), and cover to keep warm if serving soon.

VEAL RAGOUT

MEAT

MAKES 6 SERVINGS

Each fall, when the first cold snap hits, I start looking for hearty dishes with big flavor like this homey bit of French peasant artistry, named with the French term ragoûter, *or "revive the taste." The delicate veal is complemented by the flavorful herbs and cipollini onions. Recipes like this are perfect for the slow cooker—all the way through early spring. The longer the ingredients "hang out" together, the better the flavor. Each ingredient has the time it needs to flavor and perfume the entire mix. I like to serve ragout with a mix of seasonal squashes, which soak up the veal's sauce without overpowering the dish.*

The veal can be made 3 days ahead of serving and can be stored, covered, in the refrigerator, or frozen for up to 1 month. To reheat gently, preheat the oven to 300°F. Place the ragout in a casserole and cover. Reheat in the oven for 15 to 20 minutes.

Olive oil

3 pounds veal shoulder, cut into 2-inch cubes

Kosher salt and freshly ground black pepper

2 tablespoons Herbes de Provence (page 196)

½ cup all-purpose flour

10 cipollini onions, peeled (see page 115)

4 medium shallots, cut in half

2 medium carrots, peeled and diced

1 medium fennel bulb, trimmed, cored, and diced

4 garlic cloves, chopped

2 cups Essential Chicken Stock (page 207)

2 tablespoons tomato paste

2 ounces (½ cup) dried porcini mushrooms

1 bay leaf

1 cup dry white wine such as chardonnay

SUGGESTED GARNISHES

Chopped fresh sage leaves, chopped fresh flat-leaf parsley

SUGGESTED ACCOMPANIMENTS

Herbed Winter Squash (page 143), potatoes

1. Preheat a slow cooker to Low. Place a large sauté pan over medium-high heat. Lightly coat the bottom of the pan with oil.

2. Season the veal with salt and pepper. Mix the Herbes de Provence and flour together in a medium bowl. Dredge the veal in the flour mixture. Brown the veal in the sauté pan on all sides, in batches, adding more oil if necessary to prevent the veal from sticking, 5 to 7 minutes. Transfer the veal to the slow cooker insert.

3. Add the onions and shallots to the sauté pan. Cook until they are quite brown and fragrant, about 15 minutes. Transfer the onions to the insert.

4. Add the carrots and fennel to the sauté pan and cook until they are lightly colored, 5 to 7 minutes. Add the garlic and cook for 3 minutes more, until the garlic is very fragrant and slightly softened. Transfer the carrots, fennel, and garlic to the insert.

5. Raise the heat under the sauté pan, pour in the chicken stock, and bring to a simmer, scraping up with a wooden spatula any browned bits (*sucs*; see page 7) that have stuck to the pan. Transfer the liquid to the insert.

6. Add the tomato paste, dried mushrooms, bay leaf, and wine to the insert. Cover and cook on Low for 6 hours or on High for 4 hours until the meat is tender.

7. Serve the ragout with Herbed Winter Squash or your favorite potato dish. Ladle the veal and the braising liquid into a large bowl or deep platter. Sprinkle with the sage and parsley.

LAMB TAGINE

MAKES 6 TO 8 SERVINGS

I have made and served lamb tagine to thousands of customers over the last ten years in my restaurants. It has been so popular that it became my signature dish. I love the whole process of putting together my spice mix, browning the meat, and finally enjoying the big "ta-DAH!" as I remove the tagine cover and the first whiff of pure heaven wafts through the air. (I had a waiter who suggested that I should come up with a lamb tagine–scented candle.)

This dish is perfect for a special Friday night dinner, a Sunday feast, or for any festive meal. The tagine is also economical. The vegetables and dried fruit "grow" the inexpensive cut of lamb into an exotic concoction. Using the slow cooker to prepare it helps make it a dish even the cook can enjoy. Lamb tagine can be made and stored, covered, in the refrigerator for up to 2 days, or frozen for up to 1 month. To reheat gently, preheat the oven to 300°F. Place the tagine in a casserole and cover. Reheat in the oven for 15 to 20 minutes.

3 pounds lamb shoulder, cut into 2-inch cubes
Kosher salt and freshly ground black pepper

Olive oil

2 large Spanish onions, diced

6 medium carrots, peeled and cut into large dice

2 medium fennel bulbs, trimmed, cored, and diced (reserve the fronds for garnish)

8 large garlic cloves, chopped

½ cup halved pitted dates

½ cup halved dried figs

½ cup halved dried apricots

2 heaping tablespoons tomato paste

3 tablespoons Moroccan Spice Mix (page 201)

2 tablespoons charnushka (optional; see Note, page 109)

3 to 4 cups Essential Chicken Stock (page 207) or water

SUGGESTED GARNISHES

Preserved Lemons (page 213), rind only, rinsed and sliced into thin strips; Harissa (page 181); chopped cilantro; Charmoula (page 187)

SUGGESTED ACCOMPANIMENT

Steamed couscous

1. Preheat a 6½-quart slow cooker to Low.

2. Place the lamb chunks on a sheet pan or cutting board. Pat the meat dry with paper towels; this will ensure even browning. Season the lamb with salt and pepper. Place a large sauté pan over medium heat. Lightly coat the bottom of the pan with olive oil. Brown the lamb pieces on all sides, in batches, 5 to 7 minutes. Transfer the lamb to the slow cooker insert.

3. Brown the onions in batches in the sauté pan, scraping up any browned bits (*sucs*; see page 7) left behind from the lamb. Transfer the onions to the insert.

4. Sauté the carrots and fennel until they are lightly browned, about 5 minutes. Add the garlic and cook for 1 minute more. Be careful not to let the garlic brown. Transfer the vegetables to the insert.

5. Add the dates, figs, apricots, tomato paste, spice mix, and charnushka (if using) to the insert. Add stock to cover. Cover and cook on Low for 4 hours, until the lamb is tender and the sauce has thickened.

6. Serve as is or with your choice of garnishes.

MOROCCAN FEAST

Making Lamb Tagine is more than making dinner. The exotic fragrances and rich texture of the tagine juices make this dish more than a meal—it is indeed a feast. With the slow cooker helping to make the tagine easy to "throw together," I like to round out the meal by pairing the sensuous concoction with some simple side dishes. Of course, you can serve the Lamb Tagine with some easy couscous and still impress your family and friends. But why stop there? I like to serve my tagine with a variety of salads and garnishes including Sweet Potato Salad with Preserved Lemons and Olives (page 145). The bright orange potatoes and tangy olives are the perfect foil for the rich tagine. I also like to offer Carrots with Dried Currants (page 148) and small bowls of garlicky-hot Harissa (page 181) and citrusy Charmoula (page 187). These simple do-ahead condiments allow diners to customize their meal. The flavors of these dishes harmonize with the lamb and add textural interest.

My idea for this feast is to dress your table with your brightest linens, scatter bowls of sauces, couscous, sweet potato salad, and, of course, the tagine on the table, and let your friends and family truly feast on an abundant and well-prepared meal. With your slow cooker by your side, you will hardly break a sweat.

Poultry Entrées

Beef, veal, and lamb are not the only proteins that benefit from a long, slow session in the slow cooker. Chicken and turkey are delicately flavored and provide the perfect canvas to "paint" upon with richly flavored braising liquids, zesty spice mixtures, and earthy herbs. Exceptional flavor and texture are the result from poultry being cooked in the slow cooker. Recipes that I would not even attempt on a weeknight, that require hours of time, a day off, or my entire culinary staff can be had with some planning, a bit of prep, and a slow cooker.

CHICKEN WITH RICE

MEAT

MAKES 4 TO 5 SERVINGS

I love saffron's sharp, pungent smell and bright egg-yolk color. I also love how even a dish as simple as chicken and rice is transformed into a special meal by adding this exotic spice. I always make this dish with brown rice because it retains its al dente texture even after a long, slow cook, allowing for a pleasing balance of textures.

Olive oil

8 bone-in, skin-on chicken thighs

Kosher salt and freshly ground black
    pepper

2 large Spanish onions, thinly sliced

2 red bell peppers, roasted (see page 37),
    stemmed, seeded, peeled, and cut
    into thin strips

4 garlic cloves, chopped

1 cup dry white wine such as pinot grigio

2 cups Essential Chicken Stock (page 207)

2 tablespoons tomato paste

½ teaspoon saffron threads

½ teaspoon pimenton (see Note, page 65)

½ teaspoon chili flakes (optional)

2 cups short-grain brown rice

One 28-ounce can whole peeled plum
    tomatoes with their juices, crushed
    (see page 8)

½ cup chopped fresh flat-leaf parsley

1. Preheat a slow cooker to Low. Place a large sauté pan over medium heat. Lightly coat the bottom of the pan with olive oil. Pat the chicken thighs dry with paper towels. Lightly salt and pepper the chicken. Cook the chicken, skin side down, in batches, until thoroughly browned, about 10 minutes. Turn the thighs and brown the other side. Set the chicken pieces aside.

2. Drain off all but 2 tablespoons of the fat from the sauté pan. Return the pan to medium heat. Brown the onions about 12 minutes. Add the peppers and cook until they are slightly soft, about 3 minutes. Add the garlic and cook for 3 minutes more, until the garlic is very fragrant and slightly softened. Add the white wine and scrape up the browned bits (*sucs*; see page 7). Add the stock, tomato paste, saffron, pimenton, and chili flakes (if using). Stir to combine. Transfer to the insert.

3. Stir the rice and the tomatoes with their juices into vegetables in the insert. Place the chicken on top and add any juices that have accumulated. Cover and cook on Low for 6 hours.

4. Gently remove the chicken pieces and mound on a platter with the rice and vegetables. Sprinkle with the parsley.

N O T E

▶ Pimenton is a Spanish smoked paprika. It is really not comparable to the paprika found in most grocery stores. It may be sweet or hot, and has a wonderful smokiness essential to paella, chorizo, and other Spanish delicacies. Pimenton can be found in some well-stocked supermarkets, online, or at specialty markets (see Sources, page 233).

MOROCCAN CHICKEN WITH CRACKED GREEN OLIVES AND PRESERVED LEMONS

MEAT

MAKES 6 SERVINGS

The piquant mixture of silky-fragrant preserved lemons and tart olives in this dish make a regular chicken dinner taste exciting. Cracked green olives are cured with garlic and spices. The olive is lightly smashed so that the flesh marinates in the tasty brine. Use the best-quality olives you can find. Cracked green olives are easily found in many grocery stores, Middle Eastern markets, and online (see Sources, page 233). I like to serve this with a heaping bowl of couscous to soak up all the tasty juices.

Two 4-pound chickens, cut into 6 pieces
  each
Kosher salt and freshly ground black
  pepper
Olive oil
3 large Spanish onions, thinly sliced
2 medium fennel bulbs, trimmed, cored,
  and thinly sliced
1 head of garlic, separated into cloves,
  peeled, and chopped
1 cup cracked green olives, pitted

2 Preserved Lemons (page 213), rinsed,
  flesh discarded, rind thinly sliced
1 tablespoon fennel seeds
2 teaspoons ground turmeric
1 teaspoon saffron threads
2 teaspoons charnushka (see Note)
3 teaspoons chili flakes (optional)
2 cups Essential Chicken Stock (page 207)

SUGGESTED GARNISHES
Chopped fresh flat-leaf parsley, chopped
fresh cilantro

SUGGESTED ACCOMPANIMENTS
Couscous (page 141)

1 Preheat a slow cooker to Low. Pat the chicken pieces dry with paper towels. Lightly season them with salt and pepper.

2 Place a large sauté pan over medium-high heat. Lightly coat the bottom of the pan with olive oil. Cook the chicken pieces, in batches, until thoroughly browned, 7 to 10 minutes per side, to add depth to the dish. Transfer the chicken pieces to the slow cooker insert.

3. Add the onions to the sauté pan and cook over medium-high heat until browned and soft, about 10 minutes. Transfer the onions to the insert.

4. Add the sliced fennel to the sauté pan and cook until lightly browned and softened, about 10 minutes. Add the garlic to the fennel and cook for 2 minutes more. Transfer the fennel and garlic to the insert.

5. Add the olives, preserved lemon rind, fennel seeds, turmeric, saffron, charnushka, chili flakes (if using), and stock to the insert. Cover and cook on Low for 6 hours.

6. Transfer the chicken and sauce to a serving platter or bowl. Sprinkle with chopped parsley and cilantro. Serve with couscous.

NOTE

▶ *Charnushka*, a slightly smoky, pungent spice, is also called black caraway, nigella, and kalonji. It is not, however, the same thing as black cumin. Charnushka is commonly found in Middle Eastern cuisines as well as Indian spice mixes such as garam masala. Look for it in well-stocked markets or specialty stores (see Sources, page 233).

SZECHWAN CHICKEN WITH STAR ANISE SAUCE

MAKES 6 SERVINGS

Even if this dish seems a bit unusual, the deep licorice and warm brandy flavors combine with the sugar and orange in an intoxicating combination. Even if this dish seems a bit unusual at first glance, beware: It can be addictive. The deep licorice and warm brandy flavors combine with the sugar and orange in an intoxicating combination.

Szechwan peppercorns are actually the bud of a tiny fruit. They are not peppery hot like white or black peppercorns. Instead, they have a lemony flavor. Szechwan peppercorns are commonly used in many Chinese dishes and are often found with star anise and ginger in recipes. Star anise is from a Chinese evergreen tree and has a deep licorice flavor that is delicious with poultry and fish.

I prefer leaving the bones and skin on for this preparation as the flavor will be richer and deeper. You do not need salt as kosher chicken and the soy sauce are both salty.

2 teaspoons Szechwan peppercorns (see Sources, page 233)

6 pieces star anise (see Sources, page 233)

6 whole black peppercorns (about ¼ teaspoon)

One 3-inch cinnamon stick

Canola oil

2 chickens, each about 3½ pounds and cut into 6 pieces

Freshly ground black pepper

1 medium Spanish onion, chopped

6 large garlic cloves, peeled and crushed

¼ cup coarsely chopped peeled fresh ginger

1½ cups Essential Chicken Stock (page 207)

1 serrano chile, seeded and coarsely chopped

1 cup regular soy sauce

2 tablespoons tomato paste

2 unpeeled oranges, sliced

½ cup orange-flavored liqueur

1 cup brandy

½ cup light brown sugar

½ cup cornstarch

½ cup water

6 scallions, sliced

Candied Kumquats (page 157), steamed white or brown rice

1. Preheat a slow cooker to Low. Place a large heavy sauté pan over medium-high heat. Toast the Szechwan peppercorns, star anise, black peppercorns, and cinnamon stick in the pan until they are fragrant and have darkened slightly, 3 to 5 minutes. Transfer the spices to the slow cooker insert.

2. Turn down the heat under the sauté pan to medium and lightly coat the bottom of the pan with canola oil. Pat the chicken pieces dry with paper towels. Season them with pepper. Cook the chicken, in batches, until browned and caramelized on all sides, about 7 minutes per side. Transfer the chicken to the insert.

3. Add the onion to the sauté pan. Cook until browned and very soft, about 15 minutes. Add the garlic and ginger. Cook for several minutes until the garlic has softened slightly. With a slotted spoon, transfer the onion mixture to the insert.

4. Add the stock, serrano chile, soy sauce, tomato paste, orange slices, liqueur, brandy, and brown sugar to the insert. Stir to combine. Place the chicken on top and add any juices that have accumulated. Cover and cook on Low for 3 hours, until the chicken is cooked through.

5. Gently remove the chicken pieces and set aside to keep warm. Pour the braising liquid through a fine-mesh strainer into a medium saucepan and discard the solids. Skim off any excess fat.

6. Stir the cornstarch into the water to dissolve. Stir the mixture into the braising liquid. Simmer the sauce for 30 minutes. Adjust the seasoning with soy sauce and ground white pepper.

7. Sprinkle with the sliced scallions. Serve the chicken with the sauce, rice, and Candied Kumquats.

VARIATION

You can also serve this dish as an appetizer—simply substitute 7 pounds of chicken wings for the cut-up chickens and reduce the cooking time to 2 hours.

SPICY CHICKEN MEATBALLS

MEAT

MAKES 6 MAIN-COURSE SERV-INGS OR 12 SOUP GARNISHES

If you're looking for a creative way to serve these meatballs as a main course, try tucking a few inside a hot dog roll—simple, satisfying, and economical. These flavor-packed nuggets are also a hearty addition to Chick Pea and Lentil Soup (page 35) and also make for an exotic first course.

The meatballs can be made 3 days ahead and can be stored, covered, in the refrigerator, or frozen for up to 1 month.

2 pounds ground chicken

¼ cup fresh bread crumbs (leftover challah works well)

¼ cup cooked basmati rice, cooled

2 large eggs, whisked

3 tablespoons chicken fat or olive oil

¼ cup Moroccan Spice Mix (page 201)

1 medium Spanish onion, grated with a Microplane or on a box grater

3 garlic cloves, grated with a Microplane or on the fine side of a box grater

¼ cup chopped fresh flat-leaf parsley

2 tablespoons chopped fresh cilantro

2 tablespoons chopped fresh savory or 1 tablespoon fresh thyme leaves

2 tablespoons Harissa (page 181; optional)

Kosher salt and freshly ground black pepper

Olive oil

5 cups Essential Chicken Stock (page 207)

1. Combine the ground chicken, bread crumbs, rice, eggs, chicken fat, spice mix, onion, garlic, parsley, cilantro, savory, harissa, 1 tablespoon salt, and 2 teaspoons pepper in a large bowl. Gently mix everything with your hands.

2. Place a large sauté pan over medium heat. Lightly coat the bottom of the pan with olive oil. Form a teaspoon-sized meatball. (This is your test meatball to make sure the seasoning is correct.) Cook the meatball until it is cooked through. Taste for salt and pepper and adjust if necessary. Turn off the heat under the sauté pan.

3. Form meatballs in the desired size: Use a melon baller to form small soup-sized balls or an ice cream scoop for main course–sized balls. You can also lightly moisten your hands with water and roll the ingredients between your fingertips, not palms, keeping your touch light. Do not press the ingredients together or the meatballs will be tough.

4. Reheat the sauté pan over medium heat. Brown the meatballs in batches, about 5 minutes per batch, adding more oil if necessary. Transfer the meatballs to a slow cooker insert.

5. Add the chicken stock, cover, and cook on Low for 4 hours for large meatballs and 3 hours for smaller meatballs. The braising liquid that the meatballs cooked in is tasty and can be served with them as a delicious soup.

COQ AU VIN

MAKES 4 SERVINGS

The deep, earthy flavor and fragrance of the porcini mushroom powder complements the wine and herbs perfectly in this chicken and wine stew. This is a terrific example of a recipe that is enhanced by the slow cooker—it just gets better the more time the ingredients mingle. I prefer using the slow cooker for this even when I have time to tend the pot. The flavors are deeper and more layered when made in the slow cooker.

Olive oil

8 ounces cremini mushrooms, quartered

8 skin-on, bone-in chicken thighs

Kosher salt and freshly ground black pepper

¼ cup all-purpose flour

2 tablespoons Porcini Dust (page 202)

1 large Spanish onion, chopped

2 medium shallots, chopped

2 medium carrots, peeled and chopped

2 celery stalks, chopped

6 garlic cloves, chopped

1 bottle (750 ml) dry red wine such as pinot noir

3 tablespoons tomato paste

1 cup Essential Chicken Stock (page 207)

Bouquet garni of 6 thyme sprigs, 1 bay leaf, and 6 parsley sprigs, tied together with kitchen twine

3 cups pearl onions (about ¾ pound), peeled and sautéed (see page 115)

SUGGESTED ACCOMPANIMENTS

Mashed potatoes, garlic-roasted potatoes, steamed rice, pasta, toasted baguette slices rubbed with olive oil and garlic

1. Preheat a slow cooker to Low. Place a large sauté pan over medium-high heat. Lightly coat the bottom of the pan with olive oil. Cook the mushrooms until they are browned and very fragrant, about 5 minutes. Reserve the mushrooms in a covered container. Turn off the heat under the sauté pan.

2. Pat the chicken pieces dry with paper towels. Lightly season the chicken with salt and pepper. Mix together the flour and porcini dust. Dredge the chicken pieces in the flour mixture. Return the sauté pan to medium heat and add more oil if necessary. Brown the chicken pieces, in batches, on both sides, about 7 minutes per side. Transfer

each batch of chicken to the insert. When all of the chicken has been browned, drain off all but 2 tablespoons of the fat.

3. Cook the onion, shallots, carrots, and celery in the sauté pan, in batches, until the vegetables are lightly colored, about 5 minutes per batch. Season each batch with salt and pepper. Add the garlic to the last batch and cook for 3 minutes more until the garlic is very fragrant and has softened slightly. Transfer each batch of vegetables to the insert.

4. Increase the heat under the sauté pan to medium-high and add the wine. Scrape up any browned bits (sucs; see page 7) with a wooden spoon. Transfer the wine to the insert. Add the tomato paste, stock, and bouquet garni to the insert. Stir to combine. Cover and cook on Low for 8 hours, until the chicken is very tender.

5. Gently remove the chicken pieces to a serving platter and set aside to keep warm, tented with foil. Pour the braising liquid through a fine-mesh strainer into a large saucepan. Press on the vegetables to get all of the liquid, then discard the vegetables. Skim off and discard the fat. Bring the liquid to a boil, then simmer until about 2 cups remain.

6. Add the pearl onions and mushrooms to the sauce to warm them. Spoon the sauce over the chicken and serve with your choice of accompaniment.

VARIATION

You can enjoy this elegant dinner any night of the week. The pearl onions and mushrooms can be cooked up to 2 days ahead and stored, covered, in the refrigerator. The chicken and vegetables can be browned, combined with the other ingredients, and stored, covered, overnight in the refrigerator in a Dutch oven or casserole. (Do not store the ingredients in the slow cooker insert.)

The next day, transfer the ingredients to the insert. Allow the ingredients to come to room temperature before cooking. Continue with the recipe as written.

HOW TO PEEL AND SAUTÉ PEARL ONIONS

Peeling tiny pearl onions can be frustrating enough to make you swear off using them, unless you do the following: Bring a pot of water to a boil. Blanch the onions for 1 minute and then immediately plunge them into cold water. Drain the onions, cut off the root end, and the peel will easily slide off. To give the onions a gorgeous brown color and caramelized flavor, sauté them in olive oil or butter over medium heat until they are golden, about 5 minutes.

My favorite cipollini onions can be treated exactly the same way for a fast and easy side dish or addition to braised dishes.

CURRIED CHICKEN

MEAT

MAKES 5 TO 6 SERVINGS

The exotic flavors of curry are perfect for a long slow-cooked treatment. The spices, garlic, onions, and coconut milk all have time to meld resulting in one delicious, fragrant meal.

Olive oil

2 chickens, each about 3½ pounds and cut into 6 pieces, or 12 pieces skin-on, bone-in chicken (about 7 pounds)

Kosher salt and freshly ground black pepper

2 large Spanish onions, chopped

3 medium carrots, peeled and chopped

6 garlic cloves, chopped

1½ cups Essential Chicken Stock (page 207)

One 13.5- to 14-ounce can unsweetened coconut milk

3 tablespoons Curry Powder (page 198)

½ cup chopped tomatoes with juice, fresh or canned

2 cups fresh or frozen sweet peas, preferably petits pois, thawed if frozen

1 cup green lentils (see Sources, page 233)

SUGGESTED GARNISHES

Chopped fresh flat-leaf parsley, chopped fresh cilantro, fresh lime juice

SUGGESTED ACCOMPANIMENTS

Brown Basmati Rice (page 140)

1. Preheat a slow cooker to Low. Place a large sauté pan over medium-high heat. Lightly coat the bottom of the pan with oil.

2. Pat the chicken pieces dry and season with salt and pepper. Cook the chicken pieces, in batches, until browned, about 7 minutes per side. Transfer to the slow cooker insert.

3. Pour off the excess fat from the sauté pan. Brown the onions and carrots in batches, 5 to 7 minutes per batch. Season with salt and pepper. Add the garlic to the last batch of vegetables and continue to cook for 3 minutes more, until the garlic is very fragrant and has softened slightly. Transfer the vegetables to the insert.

4. Add the stock, coconut milk, curry powder, and tomatoes with their juices to the insert. Cover and cook on High for 2 hours.

5. Add the peas and lentils. Cover and cook for 1 hour more, until the lentils are cooked through but still al dente.

6. Ladle the chicken and vegetables over Brown Basmati Rice in bowls and garnish with herbs and fresh lime juice.

BRAISED TURKEY BREAST
IN MOLE POBLANO

MAKES 8 TO 10
GENEROUS SERVINGS

*This small feast works equally well as an
impressive entrée for Thanksgiving or Sukkot
(the Jewish harvest holiday), or as a nourishing
weeknight meal. To save time, I often make a
double batch of the mole and freeze half. With
the mole (MÓ-lay) ready, the dish is a snap to
put together. The sliced breast on a platter with
this gorgeous brick red–colored mole makes a
great presentation.*

*I like to use the slow cooker for cooking
turkey and other poultry. Turkey breast is
always challenging to cook as it tends to dry
out easily. The slow cooker keeps the breast
moist and juicy. The turkey can be stored in the
sauce, covered, in the refrigerator for up to 3
days.*

Olive oil

**Kosher salt and freshly ground black
pepper**

**One 4- to 5-pound skin-on boneless
turkey breast, cut in half along the
breastbone**

3 to 4 cups Mole Poblano (recipe follows)

MEAT

SUGGESTED GARNISHES
Sesame seeds, chopped fresh flat-leaf parsley,
chopped fresh cilantro or cilantro sprigs

SUGGESTED ACCOMPANIMENTS
Mashed Sweet Potatoes (page 155), brown
rice, roasted potatoes

1. Preheat a 6½-quart slow cooker to Low.
2. Place a large sauté pan over medium-high
   heat. Lightly coat the bottom of the pan
   with oil. Salt and pepper the turkey breast.
   Brown the breast halves one at a time on
   the skin side until the skin is deeply browned
   and crispy, about 10 minutes. Transfer the
   breast halves to the slow cooker insert.
3. Add the mole poblano. Cover and cook on
   Low for 4 to 5 hours, depending upon how
   much the turkey breast weighed. The larger
   the breast, the longer it will take.
4. Remove the turkey breast halves from the
   slow cooker. Slice crosswise with a very
   sharp knife. Place the slices on a platter and
   ladle the sauce over the turkey. Garnish
   with sesame seeds, chopped parsley, and
   cilantro. Serve the turkey with your choice
   of accompaniments.

continues

MOLE POBLANO

MAKES ABOUT 2 QUARTS

If you have never tried a mole, now is the time. The complex, layered flavors—fragrant spices, earthy chiles, and velvety chocolate—can bring any main course to life. Making a mole will also test any cook's mettle; it requires organization, timing, and several cooking methods. While I am a fan of quick dinners, I know that sometimes a great dish cannot rushed. I often crave slow-cooked sauces with layer upon layer of flavor. This sauce is an example of the type of flavors I long for. So I get myself organized and dig in. Once all of the ingredients are prepped, the slow cooker will do the rest.

I always find my ingredients at Latin markets. Recently I noticed that my local organic grocery store started carrying large quantities of chiles and other Latin ingredients. The chiles are usually packaged in large bags. "Fresh" dried chiles should be soft and very pliable—like a raisin—with a deep color. They should smell very earthy. The chiles in this recipe are not spicy hot, but have a complex, rich, sweet-zippy flavor.

A deep-fry or candy thermometer will help you for this recipe. The mole can be stored, covered, in the refrigerator for up to 5 days, or frozen for up to 3 months.

20 dried mulato chiles (see Sources, page 233)

8 dried ancho chiles (see Sources, page 233)

Neutral-flavored oil such as canola

½ cup raw unblanched almonds

½ cup dark raisins

½ cup pepitas (pumpkin seeds)

2 corn tortillas

2 slices of stale white bread

1 medium Spanish onion, chopped

6 garlic cloves, chopped

¼ cup sesame seeds

1 avocado leaf (see Sources, page 233)

One 3-inch cinnamon stick

½ teaspoon whole black peppercorns

½ teaspoon coriander seeds

¼ teaspoon anise seeds

2 cups drained canned whole peeled plum tomatoes (see page 8)

8 cups Essential Chicken Stock (page 207), Turkey Stock (page 209), or Vegetable Stock (page 211)

4 ounces bittersweet chocolate such as Callebaut, grated or finely chopped

1 tablespoon kosher salt

1 teaspoon freshly ground black pepper

½ cup sugar

1. Line a sheet pan with several layers of paper towels or with clean brown paper bags. Stem and seed the chiles. Reserve the seeds; you will need ¼ cup.

2. Heat at least 2 inches of oil in a large heavy saucepan or Dutch oven to 350°F. Fry the chiles in small batches until they have darkened, about 10 seconds. Remove the chiles with a wire skimmer and drain them on the sheet pan. Set aside the pan with the oil. After the chiles have cooled, place them in a large bowl, cover with water, and soak until they have softened, about 1 hour.

3. While the chiles are soaking, bring the oil back up to 350°F. Fry the almonds until they are browned, about 1 minute. Remove with the wire skimmer and place on the sheet pan to drain. Fry the raisins until they are puffed, about 30 seconds. Remove with the wire skimmer and place on the sheet pan to drain. Fry the pepitas until they begin to pop, about 20 seconds. Remove with the wire skimmer and place on the sheet pan to drain. Fry the tortillas and bread until they are both browned and crispy, about 1 minute. Remove with the wire skimmer and place on the sheet pan to drain. Add the onion and garlic and fry until browned, about 3 minutes. Pour the onion mixture and oil through a fine-mesh strainer into a heatproof container. Set aside the onion. Let the oil cool completely and discard it. Wipe out the pan and set it aside for later.

4. In a small dry sauté pan over medium-high heat, toast the reserved chile seeds until they are very fragrant and have darkened, 2 to 3 minutes. Transfer the seeds to a plate to cool. Toast the sesame seeds until golden, about 1 minute. Transfer to the plate to cool. Toast the avocado leaf, cinnamon stick, peppercorns, and coriander and anise seeds until fragrant and lightly colored, about 3 minutes. Transfer to the plate to cool. Process all the toasted ingredients in a spice grinder until finely ground.

5. Remove the chiles from the water and reserve the water. Combine the chiles, almonds, raisins, pepitas, tortillas, bread, onion-garlic mixture, ground spice, and tomatoes in a large bowl. Puree the ingredients in small batches in a blender or food processor. (You may need to break up the tortillas and bread into smaller pieces first.) Use the reserved chile soaking liquid as necessary to help puree the mix.

6. Pass the puree through a fine-mesh strainer or food mill. (This ensures a velvety mole.)

7. Place the saucepan or Dutch oven over medium-high heat. Lightly coat the bottom with oil. Lightly brown the paste. Transfer the paste to the insert of a 6½-quart slow cooker. Stir in the stock, chocolate, salt, pepper, and sugar.

8. Cover and cook on High for 4 hours. Adjust the seasoning and serve.

MOROCCAN-SPICED DUCK WITH SWEET-TART ORANGE SAUCE AND FORBIDDEN RICE

MEAT

MAKES 4 SERVINGS

Aigre-doux is the French term for the combined flavors of sour and sweet. Typically a sweet-tart sauce uses vinegar and sugar to achieve the desired mouth-puckering effect—but this isn't your mother's sweet-and-sour sauce. Instead, this stylish, updated version combines fragrant spices and sparkly orange and kumquat flavors with palate-pleasing brown sugar and honey. This recipe looks complicated at first but is broken down into manageable steps: The confit is made ahead of time, the spice mix is made at your leisure, and the sauce is just a quick pan sauce. Still, you will wow your family and friends with the sophisticated combination.

The duck breasts can be browned ahead and kept at room temperature for 1 hour before finishing them in the oven.

FOR THE DUCK

4 whole legs Duck Confit (page 122)
**4 skin-on, boneless raw duck breast
    halves**
¼ cup Moroccan Spice Mix (page 201)
Freshly ground black pepper

FOR THE SAUCE

**Grated zest and juice of 4 oranges
    (see Note)**
**Grated zest and juice of 1 lemon
    (see Note)**
½ cup rice vinegar
¼ cup light brown sugar
¼ cup honey
1 cup Essential Chicken Stock (page 207)
1 garlic clove, peeled and crushed
1 medium shallot, finely chopped
**Kosher salt and freshly ground black
    pepper**
**1 cup Candied Kumquats (page 157),
    sliced in half**

Forbidden Rice (recipe follows)

1. **Make the Duck.** Preheat the oven to 350°F.
2. Rub the duck legs and breasts generously with the spice mix. Lightly season the duck with freshly ground pepper. (Kosher duck can be salty and doesn't require additional salt.) Trim the excess fat off the duck breast.
3. Using a very sharp knife, score the skin on the breasts in a crosshatch pattern. (This

allows the fat to cook off and the skin to crisp up.)

4. Place the duck breasts skin side down in a large unheated ovenproof sauté pan. Place the pan over low heat. Cook the breasts until the skin is browned and most of the fat is rendered, draining off the fat from the pan as it accumulates, about 7 to 10 minutes.

5. When the breasts have browned, place the pan in the oven and roast them for about 8 minutes for medium rare, or longer for more cooked meat. Set the breasts aside to keep warm on a plate tented with foil.

6. Place the duck legs in the sauté pan skin side down and cook over medium heat until the skin has crisped and the legs are heated through, about 10 minutes.

7. **Make the Sauce.** Place the orange and lemon zest and juices, vinegar, sugar, honey, stock, garlic, and shallot in a medium saucepan. Bring to a boil and simmer until the sauce has reduced to about 1 cup, about 10 minutes.

8. Strain the sauce through a fine-mesh strainer and return it to the saucepan. Adjust the seasoning with salt and pepper. Add the kumquats, reduce the heat, and keep warm until ready to serve.

9. Mound the rice on a platter. Slice the breasts crosswise and place them on top of the rice. Surround with the duck confit and drizzle the sauce on top of the dish.

NOTE

▶ First grate the zest with a Microplane, then cut the fruit in half and squeeze the juice.

FORBIDDEN RICE

MAKES 4 SERVINGS

MEAT

This rice is dramatic in both its color and flavor. When raw, the rice is black, but it turns dark purple when cooked and smells like freshly popped corn. I buy forbidden rice in bulk at the health food store. It is also readily available in most grocery and gourmet stores and online.

> 1½ cups forbidden rice (see Sources, page 233)
> 3 cups Essential Chicken Stock (page 207)
> 2 medium shallots, chopped
> 2 thyme sprigs
> 1 bay leaf

Place the rice, stock, shallots, thyme, and bay leaf in a small slow cooker insert. Cook on High for 2 hours, until the rice is tender. Remove the thyme stems and bay leaf and stir to fluff before serving.

HOW TO COOK DUCK WITH THE COLD-PAN METHOD

The method I like most for cooking duck breasts is to start them in an unheated or "cold" pan; a heated pan causes the skin to darken too quickly before the fat has rendered off. The unheated method yields a crispy skin without excess fat, and the meat is still rare.

DUCK CONFIT

MAKES 6 SERVINGS

This delicious confit can be shredded and served on salads or in sandwiches, and as an entrée (see page 120). Kosher duck parts are hard to find, so you have to cut the duck yourself, but duck is so delicious, it's worth the extra effort.

6 whole duck legs (legs and thighs), thawed if frozen
3 tablespoons Herbes de Provence (page 196)
Freshly ground black pepper
2 cups duck fat or mixed poultry fat

1. Pat the duck legs dry with paper towels. Rub the legs with the herbs and black pepper. Refrigerate in a shallow pan, covered, for at least 4 hours or overnight.

2. Turn on a slow cooker to High and melt the duck fat in the insert. Remove the duck legs from the refrigerator and wipe off the herbs and pepper with a paper towel. Some will stick, but that is okay. Place the duck legs into the warm fat. Cover and cook on Low for 6 hours.

3. Remove the duck legs with a slotted spoon or wire strainer. Cool the fat and duck legs separately. When cool, either wrap the legs tightly in plastic and store in the freezer for up to 3 months, or place in a container, pour the fat over them, cover tightly, and store in the refrigerator for up to 1 month. I like to store the fat in a heavy plastic bag in my freezer so I can quickly scoop some out and sauté potatoes or onions in it.

4. To serve the duck on its own, place the duck legs in a sauté pan skin side down and cook over medium heat until the skin has crisped and the legs are heated through, about 10 minutes.

HOW TO CUT UP A DUCK

Place the duck, breast side up, on a cutting board, legs facing you. Locate the breastbone in the center and cut as close to the bone as possible down the entire length of the duck on each side (this helps separate the meat without cutting into it). Keep going until each breast is cut away from the bone. Then cut the piece of skin that attaches each leg to the body. Pull each leg outward to loosen it from the joint. Cut the skin on the back and snap off the thigh at the joint. Cut off the wings. Cut off excess fat and use for confit or reserve.

Fish and Vegetarian Entrées

We eat a lot of fish in our house. I love the way I can transform mild-flavored fish into a bold, distinctive ethnic dish with the addition of spices. I can change the same type of fish into a different dish by adding mushrooms and white wine. Cooking fish in the slow cooker is relatively new to me, but with some trial and error I discovered that the slow cooker is perfect. I don't have to worry about the fish becoming dry and flaky; instead it remains moist and flavorful.

SOLE WITH WHITE WINE AND MUSHROOMS

MAKES 5 TO 6 SERVINGS

The earthy mushrooms in this simple dish—called sole bonne femme *in French—combine with the white wine and cream to make their own luxurious sauce. I have served this dish during Passover and dressed it up with the addition of dried porcini mushrooms and seasonal specialties, spring onions and ramps. Ramps are wild leeks with a pungent onion-garlic flavor. They are available usually in the early spring. They are foraged and are very special. If you are lucky enough to find these treasures in your grocery store or farmers' market, add them to this versatile dish. If ramps are unavailable, no problem. The dish is equally delicious with shallots and leeks.*

DAIRY

½ cup liquid from Mushroom Duxelles (page 214)

1 ounce (¼ cup) dried porcini mushrooms (optional)

3 tablespoons (⅜ stick) unsalted butter

½ to ¾ cup Mushroom Duxelles (page 214)

¼ cup dry white wine such as chardonnay

1½ pounds fresh sole fillets (lemon, gray, or other mild-flavored sole)

3 tablespoons chopped fresh flat-leaf parsley

1 tablespoon chopped fresh thyme

1 teaspoon chopped fresh chives

1 bunch ramps *or* 2 small leeks, white parts only, thinly sliced plus 2 medium shallots, thinly sliced

¼ cup heavy cream

Kosher salt and freshly ground black
    pepper

Grated zest of 1 lemon

1 cup pearl onions (about ¼ pound),
    peeled and sautéed (see page 115)

SUGGESTED GARNISHES
Chopped fresh flat-leaf parsley

SUGGESTED ACCOMPANIMENTS
Roasted potatoes, cooked lentils

1 If using the porcini mushrooms, combine the mushroom duxelles liquid and porcini in a small saucepan. Bring to a simmer. Turn off the heat and allow the porcini mushrooms to soften, about 15 minutes.

2 Butter a slow cooker insert with 2 tablespoons of the butter. Spread the mushroom duxelles on the bottom of the insert. Add the duxelles liquid, soaked porcinis (if using), and wine. Fold the sole fillets in half lengthwise and arrange them on top of the mushroom duxelles. It is okay to overlap the fish fillets on top of each other. Sprinkle the fish with the parsley, thyme, and chives. Cover and cook on High for 90 minutes.

3 Place a small sauté pan over medium heat. Melt the remaining tablespoon of butter in the pan. Add the ramps, if using, or leeks and shallots. Sauté the vegetables until they are very limp and slightly colored, 3 to 5 minutes. Set aside and keep warm.

4 Gently transfer the fish to a platter and tent loosely with foil to keep warm. Transfer the sauce with the mushroom duxelles to a saucepan over medium heat. Add the cream and bring to a simmer. Reduce the sauce by half. (Do not let the cream boil.) Adjust the seasoning with salt and pepper. Stir in the lemon zest and spoon over the fish. Garnish with the pearl onions, sautéed ramps or leeks, and parsley. Serve with your choice of accompaniment.

OLIVE OIL–POACHED HALIBUT

MAKES 6 SERVINGS

This is my favorite method of cooking halibut—it's so simple in the slow cooker. The delicate flavor of the fish is enhanced by the fruity olive oil, and the buttery texture becomes more pronounced. It is normally difficult to control the oil in this dish, as it often becomes too hot too quickly on the stovetop and in the oven. The slow cooker, on the other hand, gently heats the oil and holds it at a constant temperature. Fabulous!

6 cups extra-virgin olive oil (use the oil from Preserved Lemons, page 213)

3 whole peeled garlic cloves

6 thyme sprigs

1 medium rosemary sprig

12 large fresh basil leaves

6 whole black peppercorns (about ¼ teaspoon)

6 skinless 6-ounce halibut fillets

PAREVE

SUGGESTED GARNISHES

Chopped fresh herbs such as basil, tarragon, mint, and flat-leaf parsley

SUGGESTED ACCOMPANIMENTS

Mixed Olive Tapenade (page 18) or Sun-Dried Tomato Tapenade (page 19), Toasted Capellini (page 144), green salad lightly dressed with olive oil and lemon juice

1. Preheat a slow cooker to Low. Place the oil, garlic, thyme, rosemary, basil, peppercorns, and halibut fillets in the slow cooker insert. Keep the fish in a single layer; do not stack the fillets as they will stick together.

2. Cover and cook on Low for 3 hours, until the fish is firm and cooked through.

3. Gently remove the fish with a slotted spatula. Strain the oil and store, covered, in the refrigerator. The oil may used up to three times for poaching fish.

4. Garnish with chopped herbs and serve with your choice of accompaniment.

HALIBUT INVOLTINI

PAREVE

MAKES 4 SERVINGS

Involtini *are Italian rollups of stuffed fish, veal, poultry, beef, or vegetables. When my son Jonah first tried it and exclaimed, "This dish has real 'sizzle!'" I wasn't sure if that was a good thing or not. But he quickly cleaned his plate and held it out for more. You, too, will love how each mouthful of this dish has the perfect combination of stuffing, fish, and broth.*

Olive oil

1 medium Spanish onion, thinly sliced

2 oil-packed anchovy fillets, drained and chopped

2 teaspoons chili flakes

3 garlic cloves, finely minced

2 tablespoons capers, drained and rinsed

1 cup tightly packed baby spinach

¼ cup oil-packed sun-dried tomatoes, drained and cut into thin strips

1 tablespoon tomato paste

2½ cups dry white wine such as pinot grigio

¼ cup fresh bread crumbs (leftover challah works well)

3 tablespoons chopped fresh flat-leaf parsley

Kosher salt and freshly ground black pepper

1 cup fish stock, preferably homemade, or Vegetable Stock (page 211)

2 tablespoons extra-virgin olive oil

1 teaspoon saffron threads

4 thick skinless 6-ounce halibut fillets

SUGGESTED GARNISHES

Chopped fresh flat-leaf parsley

SUGGESTED ACCOMPANIMENTS

Pasta, steamed or boiled potatoes

1 Place a large saucepan over medium-low heat. Lightly coat the bottom of the pan with olive oil. Cook the onion, stirring occasionally, until it is very soft and lightly browned, about 15 minutes. Increase the heat to medium-high. Add the anchovies and chili flakes and stir until the anchovies have melted and almost disappeared, about 1 minute. Add the garlic, capers, spinach, sun-dried tomatoes, tomato paste, ½ cup of the wine, the bread crumbs, and parsley, and cook until the mixture is very thick, about 3 minutes. Adjust the seasoning with salt and pepper. Let the stuffing cool.

2 Preheat a slow cooker to High. Combine the remaining 2 cups of wine, the stock, extra-virgin olive oil, and saffron in the slow cooker insert. Cover and heat the broth on High.

3 Butterfly the fish fillets lengthwise (see page 83), so they measure approximately 4 × 6 inches when opened. Place a small amount of stuffing (about 2 tablespoons) on each fillet. Roll up the fillets from one tip to the other and tie them snugly every 2 inches with kitchen twine.

4 Place a medium sauté pan over medium heat. Lightly coat the bottom of the pan with olive oil. Brown the rolls about 3 minutes per side. Transfer the rolls to the insert. Turn down the temperature to Low, cover, and cook on Low for 90 minutes, until the rolls are firm to the touch.

5 Gently transfer the rolls with a slotted spoon into deep soup bowls. Ladle some of the broth over the fish. Garnish with chopped parsley and serve with your choice of accompaniment.

THAI FISH WRAPPED IN BANANA LEAVES WITH JASMINE RICE

PAREVE

MAKES 6 SERVINGS

Though this is an exotic dish, it is a crowd-pleaser and simple to make. To round out the meal, serve the fish with Cucumber-Mint Relish, and pass plenty of fresh lime wedges.

3 tablespoons Thai Red Curry Paste
    (page 204; use more if you like it
    spicy as I do)

One 13.5- to 14-ounce can unsweetened
    coconut milk, plus 1 cup for the rice

2 tablespoons tomato paste

2 tablespoons regular soy sauce

2 to 3 tablespoons light brown sugar

Kosher salt and freshly ground black
    pepper

6 thick, firm 4-ounce skinless fish fillets,
    such as wild salmon, halibut, or
    grouper

1 package banana leaves (see Note)

1½ cups jasmine rice

2 cups water

SUGGESTED ACCOMPANIMENTS
Cucumber-Mint Relish (recipe follows), fresh lime wedges

1. Preheat a slow cooker to Low. Combine the curry paste, the can of coconut milk, the tomato paste, soy sauce, and brown sugar in a small saucepan over low heat and cook for 15 minutes, stirring occasionally, to allow the flavors to meld. Do not boil the sauce. Adjust the seasoning with salt and pepper. Remove from the heat and let cool completely.

2. Season the fish with salt and pepper. Cut six of the banana leaves into squares large enough to wrap completely around the fish, about a 6-inch square. Cut the remaining leaf into long, thin strips; these are the ties for the fish packages.

3. Place a fish fillet in the center of one of the squares. Spoon about 3 tablespoons of the sauce over the fish. Draw the sides and ends of the fish package leaves together. Tie the fish with the banana leaf ties. Continue until all the fish are bundled into packages. Reserve the remaining sauce to pass at the table.

4. Place the jasmine rice into the slow cooker insert. Stir together the remaining 1 cup of coconut milk and the water and pour over the rice. Place the fish packages on top of the rice. Cover and cook on Low for 90 minutes or until the rice is tender and the fish is firm to the touch.

5. Reheat the sauce in a small saucepan over low heat. Be careful not heat the sauce at too high a temperature as it can curdle. Gently remove the fish packages and place them on a platter. Ladle the rice into serving bowls. To eat the fish: snip off the tie, open up the package, and eat right off the banana leaves. Pass the sauce, cucumber-mint relish, and lime wedges.

NOTE

▶ Banana leaves are available frozen in Asian and Mexican markets. Thaw the package for several hours before separating for use. (See Sources, page 233.)

CUCUMBER-MINT RELISH

MAKES 6 SERVINGS   PAREVE

1 medium English (seedless) cucumber, peeled and sliced

½ small head of Napa cabbage, shredded (about 2 cups)

½ cup tightly packed fresh cilantro leaves

½ cup tightly packed chopped fresh mint leaves

3 tablespoons regular soy sauce

1½ tablespoons rice vinegar

Kosher salt and freshly ground black pepper

Combine the cucumber, cabbage, cilantro, mint, soy sauce, and rice vinegar in a bowl. Season to taste with salt and pepper. Serve immediately.

WILD MUSHROOM STROGANOFF

DAIRY

MAKES 6 SERVINGS

Stroganoff is a Russian dish typically made of beef cooked with sour cream, onions, and mushrooms. Here is a vegetarian version that is hearty and flavorful enough to satisfy the most enthusiastic carnivore. I use a variety of mushrooms, as each one adds a unique flavor and texture to the dish, but you can simplify it by using one type of fresh and one type of dried.

Olive oil

2 medium shallots, finely chopped

2 garlic cloves, finely chopped

8 ounces button mushrooms with their stems, sliced (4 cups), or 8 ounces cremini mushrooms with their stems, sliced (4 cups), or 4 ounces (2 cups) of each

2 ounces fresh shiitake mushroom caps, sliced (about 1 cup)

Kosher salt and freshly ground black pepper

⅓ cup dry sherry, preferably Spanish

4 ounces dried mushrooms such as porcini, chanterelle, and morels, any type or a combination

2 cups Vegetable Stock (page 211) or water

2 tablespoons (¼ stick) unsalted butter

2 tablespoons all-purpose flour

1 cup sour cream

2 tablespoons chopped fresh thyme leaves

1 tablespoon chopped fresh rosemary leaves

¼ cup chopped fresh flat-leaf parsley

SUGGESTED ACCOMPANIMENTS

Broad, flat pasta; thick slices of bread, toasted and rubbed with garlic

1. Preheat a slow cooker to Low. Place a large sauté pan over medium heat. Lightly coat the bottom of the pan with olive oil. Add the shallots and garlic and cook for about 5 minutes until they are soft and fragrant. Transfer the shallots and garlic to the slow cooker insert.

2. Add 2 tablespoons of oil to the sauté pan and increase the heat to high. Sauté the fresh mushrooms in batches until they are browned and lightly crispy, adding more oil

if necessary. Season each batch with salt and pepper. Before adding the last batch of mushrooms to the insert, turn off the heat under the sauté pan and stir in the sherry. (This will prevent the alcohol in the sherry from igniting.) Turn on the heat and cook mushroom mixture over medium heat for several minutes to burn off the alcohol. Transfer the last batch to the insert.

3 Add the dried mushrooms and the stock to the insert. Cover and cook on High for 90 minutes.

4 Ladle out and reserve about 1½ cups of the mushroom liquid from the slow cooker.

Melt the butter in a medium saucepan over medium-high heat. Whisk the flour into the butter until it forms a paste. Cook for 2 minutes to remove the starchy taste. Pour in the reserved mushroom liquid while continuing to whisk. Whisk in the sour cream until thoroughly blended. Pour the sauce into the slow cooker and add the thyme, rosemary, and parsley. Cover and cook the stroganoff for 30 minutes more, until the sauce has thickened. Adjust the seasoning with salt and pepper.

5 Ladle the stroganoff into a large bowl piled high with your choice of accompaniment.

SMOKY NAVY BEANS WITH EGGPLANT RAGÙ

PAREVE

MAKES 5 TO 6 SERVINGS

This satisfying vegetarian meal highlights the earthy essence of eggplant. I like to use navy beans for this recipe as they cook up firm and don't fall apart as easily as other white beans. They are also small, with a sweet flavor.

I like this for a Shabbat lunch as an alternative to a heavier cholent—sometimes I just want a lighter option. I also serve this tasty meal as a weeknight supper.

3 medium Italian eggplants or 6 large Japanese eggplants, cut into 1-inch-thick rounds

Kosher salt

Olive oil

2 large Spanish onions, thinly sliced

4 garlic cloves, chopped

2 cups dried navy beans, sorted through and soaked overnight

One 28-ounce can whole peeled plum tomatoes with their juices, crushed (see page 8)

3 tablespoons tomato paste

5 cups Vegetable Stock (page 211)

3 tablespoons pimenton (see Note, page 65)

2 teaspoons ground cumin

½ teaspoon saffron threads

Pinch of chili flakes

Freshly ground black pepper

SUGGESTED GARNISHES

Extra-virgin olive oil, chopped fresh flat-leaf parsley

1. Place the eggplant rounds on a sheet pan or in a colander. Generously salt them. Allow the eggplant to drain for 1 hour.

2. Rinse the eggplant rounds and squeeze out any excess juice. Pat dry with paper towels.

3. Preheat a slow cooker to High. Line a sheet pan with several layers of paper towels. Place a large sauté pan over medium-high heat. Lightly coat the bottom of the pan with olive oil. Fry the eggplant rounds, in batches if necessary, until they are browned and crispy, about 3 minutes per side. Transfer to the sheet pan to drain.

4. Add the onions to the pan and decrease the heat to medium. Cook the onions until very soft and dark brown, about 15 minutes. Add the garlic and cook for 3 minutes more, until the garlic is very fragrant and has softened slightly.

5. Transfer the eggplant, the onion mixture, beans, tomatoes and their juices, tomato paste, stock, pimenton, cumin, saffron, and chili flakes in the slow cooker insert. Cover and cook on High for 4 hours, until the beans are soft but still holding together. Adjust the seasoning with salt and pepper.

6. Ladle the ragù into deep soup bowls. Drizzle with tasty extra-virgin olive oil and sprinkle each bowl with chopped parsley.

NOTE

▶ Pimenton is a Spanish smoked paprika. It is really not comparable to the paprika found in most grocery stores. It may be sweet or hot, and has a wonderful smokiness essential to paella, chorizo, and other Spanish delicacies. Pimenton can be found online or at specialty markets (see Sources, page 233).

HOW TO CHOOSE AND PREPARE EGGPLANT

To find the best-flavored eggplant, look at the blossom end of the fruit. If the indentation is deep and elongated, it is a female eggplant and has more seeds, which can be bitter. Male eggplants have a shallow dimple and fewer seeds, and are less bitter.

Salting the eggplant (also known as purging) is an essential step to creating a great-tasting eggplant dish. While it requires an extra step, it is well worth the time in flavor and texture. The salt helps collapse the cell walls, which keeps the eggplant from absorbing too much oil during frying or sautéing. It also draws out the alkaloids that are concentrated around the seeds and can be bitter. To salt an eggplant: Sprinkle the sliced eggplant pieces generously with salt and let them sit in a colander for an hour. Rinse the eggplant to remove the salt, press to remove the excess water, then pat the eggplant dry.

BRAISED EGGS IN
SPICY TOMATO SAUCE

DAIRY

MAKES 4 SERVINGS

Eggs cooked in a well-flavored sauce is a common Mediterranean recipe called shakshuka. *The eggs really pick up the rich flavors of the sauce. This is even more delicious served with Cheesy Grits (page 147).*

Olive oil

2 cups Spicy Tomato Sauce (page 190)

8 large eggs

**¼ cup chopped fresh herbs, such as flat-
    leaf parsley, thyme, basil, chives,
    rosemary, alone or in combination**

1 tablespoon Za'atar (page 203)

**2 tablespoons grated Parmesan cheese,
    preferably Parmigiano-Reggiano**

SUGGESTED ACCOMPANIMENTS
Cheesy Grits (page 147)

1. Lightly rub the inside of a slow cooker insert with olive oil. Preheat the slow cooker to High.

2. Pour the sauce into the cooker. One at a time, crack the eggs into a small bowl and slide them into the cooker, being careful not to break the yolks.

3. Sprinkle the eggs with the herbs and za'atar and drizzle with olive oil.

4. Cook on High for 1 hour.

5. Sprinkle with the cheese and serve hot with the grits.

VARIATION

If you only have only one slow cooker, you can cook the eggs in an oven preheated to 350°F and use the cooker for the grits. If using the oven, reduce the cooking time to 15 minutes.

FAVA BEAN AND
LENTIL STEW

MAKES 4 TO 6 SERVINGS

In Egypt, ful medamas is called "everyman's breakfast, the shopkeeper's lunch, and the poor man's dinner." While I have enjoyed this earthy and healthy dish of favas and lentils for breakfast, as it is most commonly served, I now serve it at dinner, too (well, why not? I already have a slow cooker full of it!). Try topping the lentils with Olive Oil–Poached Halibut (page 125) and garnish with fresh herbs such as chopped parsley, cilantro, or basil. Or for a delicious vegetarian meal, serve the dish alongside Sweet Potato Salad with Preserved Lemons and Olives (page 145). If serving simply with garnishes, offer plenty of whole-grain flatbreads or toasted pita.

This dish is pareve, but using butter or egg as a garnish will make it dairy.

1½ cups small dried fava beans, sorted to remove any debris and soaked overnight in the refrigerator

½ cup red lentils, rinsed and sorted to remove any debris

1 medium Spanish onion, diced

PAREVE
or Dairy

1 clove garlic, finely chopped

2 medium tomatoes, chopped, or 1 cup whole plum tomatoes with their juices, crushed

4 ½ cups Vegetable Stock (page 211), or water, plus additional as needed

2 teaspoons Harissa (page 181; optional)

2 teaspoons kosher salt

SUGGESTED GARNISHES

Hot sauce, olive oil, tahini, Hummos (page 14), tomato sauce, butter, fried egg, hard-cooked egg, chick peas, green onions, toasted cumin seeds, chopped parsley, sumac

1. Preheat the slow cooker to High.
2. Drain the fava beans and transfer them to the slow cooker insert. Add all the remaining ingredients. Cover and cook on High for 2 hours.
3. Turn temperature down to Low and cook for 10 hours more. Check the consistency; it shouldn't be too thick. Add more liquid if needed to make it more "soupy." Serve in a bowl with your favorite condiments.

Side Dishes

*Cooking is like love. It should be entered
into with abandon or not at all.*

—HARRIET VAN HORNE

Side dishes fall into several categories. Sometimes a side dish
defines its partner entrée and gives it character and pizzazz. This
type of side dish is often inseparable from the entrée, as in the
case of Couscous (page 144) with Lamb Tagine (page 104). These
two menu items are made to go together and nothing else will do. Another
category of side dish is the "vehicle" with which to eat a dish. This type of
side should be tasty on its own, but its real mission is to help scoop up spoon-
fuls of sensuous sauce. One of my favorite recipes in this category is White
Bean Ragù (page 101). The creamy beans grab hold of rich osso buco gravy
and deliver it to my waiting taste buds every time.

Other times, the side dish is the star of the show and dresses up the
entrée. Peperonata (page 28) served as an appetizer or a side dish is just such
a recipe. This raucously colored side dish is an attention getter. The heady
sweet flavor of the peppers, basil, olive oil, and garlic are mouthwatering. This

137

dish needs nothing but a simple piece of fish, chicken, or beef to round out the meal.

Side dishes should always be thought out and composed. Sure, boiled pasta or rice will do the job. But why not spend a little extra time and make Brown Basmati Rice (page 140) to serve one day with Curried Chicken (page 116) and another day with Spicy Chicken Meatballs (page 112)?

Most of these dishes are intended to be served as sides. Make double batches and they can perform double duty. You can mix and match for different meals or serve them by themselves or with minor additions as mains for lunch or dinner.

Grains, Pastas, and Legumes

I am a grain and legume groupie. I love the chewy texture that al dente pasta adds to a dish, earthy lentils are my favorite no-fuss side, and whole grains find their way into nearly all of my side dishes, entrées, and even desserts. While I am devoted to eating grains and other toothsome side dishes, I don't always have time or energy to prepare them. This is where my slow cooker comes into play. I can pour my grain of choice into the cooker in the morning, add water or stock and some seasoning, and I am out the door.

As imports from other countries expand, the opportunities to experiment with exotic grains from around the world increases. I remember when brown rice was considered the "hot" grain of choice. Now there are at least four different types of brown rice in my cupboard at all times. I use grains from Italy and Ethiopia, rices from Thailand, China, and Burma. My lentil collection could rival that of most supermarkets, and I am always looking for more.

As a professional chef, I know that I can take a great piece of fish and pair it one night with a creamy risotto and with a barley pilaf the next, and have two completely different dishes.

As a kosher home cook, I realize the impact that grains have on my home menus as well. Let's face it—when it comes to protein, the kosher diet doesn't change much with the exception of some fish that come in and out of season. But clever side dishes made with grains and pastas can transform any tired piece of meat, poultry, or fish into something spectacular. Leftover pot roast takes on new life with each new side dish.

As a busy mother, I try to plan menus that help me get extra mileage out of my efforts— changing grains and legumes and the way they are used helps a lot. If I make Garlicky Pot Roast (page 68), for example, I may serve it one night with Simple Grits (page 146) and next to Kasha Varnishkes (page 154) on another. Sometimes I even make the grains perform double duty. I may make a simple brown rice dish and serve it as a side with my favorite brisket. Then later in the week, the same rice appears again in a salad or soup. I also enjoy updating classic grain dishes with special touches. My Wild Rice Pudding (page 164) is a dressed-up adaptation of the original that can be served as a warm breakfast treat or for dessert.

For Passover—the anti-grain holiday—I rely on quinoa (botanically, it's not a grain) as a staple side dish. After all, how many potatoes can one family eat? The popularity of quinoa has grown in recent years. Not only is this little seed sweet and delicate, it is also kosher for Passover according to many rabbinic authorities (check with your local rabbi). I celebrate this addition to my Passover pantry with Herbed Quinoa Pilaf (page 151) welcome side dish that doubles as a salad during the holiday or anytime.

If you are a whole grain or legume novice, I recommend trying Chicken with Rice (page 106). The flavors of the chicken, wine, and saffron infuse the rice with an exotic sweetness. If you are a die-hard grain and legume lover like me, try the Moroccan-Spiced Mixed Grain "Risotto" (page 152).

Many grocery stores now carry unusual grains and legumes. I also recommend ethnic grocery stores and markets (see Sources, page 233). Explore and enjoy.

BROWN BASMATI RICE

MAKES 8 SERVINGS

This fragrant rice dish is the perfect accompaniment to chicken or fish entrées. I like to make double batches and serve it throughout the week to dress up leftovers. Serve this fragrant rice with Meatloaf (page 96) or Garlicky Pot Roast (page 68), or make it with vegetable stock to serve with dairy meals.

The rice can be stored, covered, for up to 3 days in the refrigerator, or frozen for up to 1 month.

1 cup dried chick peas, sorted through, soaked overnight, and drained, or 3 cups canned, drained and rinsed

5 cups Essential Chicken Stock (page 207) or Vegetable Stock (page 211)

2 cups brown basmati rice

1 tablespoon Curry Powder (page 198)

1 tablespoon grated peeled fresh ginger

1 small fresh hot red chile pepper, seeded and minced (optional)

1 cup golden raisins

½ cup unblanched almonds, toasted (see page 199) and chopped

3 tablespoons chopped fresh cilantro

1. If using dried chick peas, place them in a slow cooker insert. Add the stock, cover, and cook on High for 2 hours.

2. Add the rice, curry powder, ginger, chile (if using), and raisins to the insert. If using canned chick peas, add them and the stock now. Cover and cook on High for 2 hours until the chick peas are tender and the rice is cooked through.

3. Sprinkle with the almonds and cilantro before serving.

COUSCOUS AND BEANS

This versatile side dish can be served hot or cold and keeps well, so you can make it up to three days before serving. I prefer the whole wheat variety of couscous, which can be found in most grocery stores, for the extra element of nutty flavor it adds. I serve the couscous with Lamb Tagine (page 104) and Moroccan Chicken with Cracked Green Olives and Preserved Lemons (page 108): I spoon the couscous onto a large serving platter, make a well in the center, and ladle the meat and sauce into the well. Made with water, the pareve version can go with anything.

The couscous can be stored, covered, in the refrigerator up to 3 days ahead of serving and can be reheated, covered, in a 300°F oven.

¾ cup dried chick peas, sorted through, soaked overnight, and drained

¾ cup dried fava beans, sorted through, soaked overnight, and drained

6 cups Essential Chicken Stock (page 207) or water

1½ cups couscous (regular, not instant)

5 tablespoons extra-virgin olive oil

½ cup petit green French lentils (see Sources, page 233)

½ cup chopped fresh flat-leaf parsley

¼ cup fresh lemon juice

¼ cup toasted pine nuts (see page 199)

Kosher salt and freshly ground black pepper

MEAT or Pareve

1. Place the chick peas and fava beans in a slow cooker insert. Add the stock. Cover and cook on High for 5 hours.

2. Place the couscous in a large bowl. Rub the grains with 1 tablespoon of oil. This helps to keep the couscous from clumping together. Add the couscous and lentils to the insert and cook for 1 more hour, until the chick peas and fava beans are tender.

3. Remove the couscous mixture and place in a large bowl. Stir in the parsley, lemon juice, pine nuts, and the remaining 4 tablespoons olive oil. Season with salt and pepper.

CUCUMBERS AND ORANGES IN ROSEWATER

PAREVE

MAKES 6 TO 8 SERVINGS

I like to serve this refreshing salad with rich Lamb Tagine (page 104) as a crunchy, fragrant accompaniment to the lamb's savory flavor. During the summer, add an additional touch of playfulness to the dish by including chunks of watermelon.

The salad can be stored in the refrigerator, covered, up to 1 day before serving.

2 large English (seedless) cucumbers, peeled and cut into thin half-moons

2 medium shallots, very finely chopped

2 oranges, peeled, membranes trimmed off, and cut into sections

2 teaspoons rosewater (see Note)

1 tablespoon fresh lemon juice

2 teaspoons extra-virgin olive oil

2 tablespoons chopped fresh flat-leaf parsley

½ cup diced seedless watermelon (during the summer only; optional)

1 teaspoon crushed pink peppercorns (optional; see Sources, page 233)

Kosher salt and freshly ground black pepper

Place the cucumbers, shallots, oranges, rosewater, lemon juice, olive oil, parsley, watermelon (if using), and pink peppercorns (if using) in a large bowl and gently toss together. Adjust the seasoning with salt and pepper.

NOTE

▶ Rosewater is distilled directly from roses and often used to flavor Middle Eastern desserts. It is inexpensive and available in the baking section of many grocery stores and gourmet markets. (See Sources, page 233.)

HERBED WINTER SQUASH

MAKES 6 SERVINGS

MEAT
or Pareve

Hard-shelled squash season is one of my favorite times of the year. Every fall, I discover some new variety of squash I have never seen before. Winter squash wear brightly colored "jackets" that demand attention while protecting their creamy orange flesh from the colder weather. There are many varieties of winter squash—some are very sweet, while others are mild and earthy. I love them all. Try something new and see if you don't become a fan of this autumnal treat. Use vegetable stock for a pareve version.

Olive oil

4 cups peeled, seeded, and diced winter squash, such as butternut, acorn, carnival, Hubbard, delicata, red kuri, cut large (from about 2½ pounds squash)

Kosher salt and freshly ground black pepper

¼ cup shallots, finely chopped (about 6 medium shallots)

2 cups Essential Chicken Stock (page 207) or Vegetable Stock (page 211)

Grated zest of 1 orange

One 2- to 3-inch cinnamon stick

½ teaspoon freshly grated nutmeg

1 whole clove

2 tablespoons chopped fresh sage

2 tablespoons chopped fresh flat-leaf parsley

2 teaspoons chopped fresh thyme

① Place a large sauté pan over medium-high heat. Lightly coat the bottom of the pan with oil. Brown the squash in batches until it is golden brown on all sides, about 5 minutes. Season each batch with salt and pepper. Transfer the squash to a slow cooker insert.

② Cook the shallots in the sauté pan until lightly browned, about 3 minutes, adding more oil if necessary. Transfer the shallots to the insert.

③ Add the stock, orange zest, cinnamon stick, nutmeg, and clove to the insert. Cover and cook on Low for 6 hours or High for 3 hours until the squash is tender.

④ Remove the cinnamon and the clove (if found). Transfer the squash to a serving bowl and sprinkle on the sage, parsley, and thyme.

TOASTED CAPELLINI (ANGEL HAIR)

MEAT
or Pareve

MAKES 6 SERVINGS

Toasting the pasta in this dish before putting it in the slow cooker gives it an incredibly nutty flavor and color. The addition of gooey caramelized onions completes this comforting side dish. I always make a large batch and reheat the leftovers for a quick weeknight meal. I serve this with Garlicky Pot Roast (page 68) and Falling-off-the-Bone Short Ribs (page 88). Use vegetable stock or water for a pareve version.

The pasta can be stored, covered, in the refrigerator for up to 3 days. To reheat gently, preheat the oven to 300°F. Place the pasta in a casserole, add a little chicken stock or water, and cover. Reheat in the oven for 15 to 20 minutes.

Olive oil

2 medium Spanish onions, thinly sliced

2 garlic cloves, minced

½ pound capellini, broken into 2- to 3-inch pieces

2 cups Essential Chicken Stock (page 207), Vegetable Stock (page 211), or water

¼ cup chopped fresh flat-leaf parsley

Kosher salt and freshly ground black pepper

1. Place a large sauté pan over medium heat. Lightly coat the bottom of the pan with olive oil. Cook the onions until they are very soft and golden brown, about 15 minutes. Add the garlic and cook for about 3 minutes, until the garlic has softened. Transfer the onions to a slow cooker insert.

2. Add more olive oil to recoat the bottom of the sauté pan and toast the pasta over medium heat about 5 minutes, until the pasta is lightly browned and has a nutty fragrance. Transfer the pasta to the insert. Stir in the stock. Cover and cook on High for 90 minutes until most of the liquid has been absorbed.

3. Turn off the cooker and allow the pasta to sit about 10 minutes, so the remaining liquid can be absorbed. Stir in the parsley and adjust the seasoning with salt and pepper. Serve the pasta warm.

SWEET POTATO SALAD WITH PRESERVED LEMONS AND OLIVES

MAKES 8 SERVINGS

PAREVE

This potato salad is a welcome addition to your table all year-round. I love using sweet potatoes in unexpected ways—in this dish, they add an extra earthy sweetness you don't find in traditional potato salad.

While I enjoy using sweet potatoes for many recipes, I don't always have the time to cook them. Really large potatoes take "forever" to cook in an oven. I found that cooking them in the slow cooker not only is easier and doesn't require my presence; it also keeps the potatoes moist and tender. The skin just slides off after cooking and the potato is ready to be turned into this brightly colored salad.

I serve this salad with Lamb Tagine (page 104) and Garlicky Pot Roast (page 68), warm or at room temperature. It can be stored, covered, in the refrigerator for up to 3 days.

2 medium carrots, peeled and diced large

3 large unpeeled sweet potatoes

Olive oil

1 teaspoon cumin seed, toasted (see page 199)

1 medium red onion, thinly sliced

Rind of 1 Preserved Lemon (page 213), rinsed and cut into very thin strips

½ cup chopped pitted green olives

1 medium fennel bulb, trimmed, cored, and very thinly sliced (reserve the fronds)

¼ cup fresh lemon juice

¼ cup extra-virgin olive oil

Kosher salt and freshly ground black pepper

① Place the carrots into a slow cooker insert.

② Rub the sweet potatoes with olive oil. Place the potatoes on top of the carrots. Cover and cook on High for 3 hours, just until the potatoes can be pierced with a paring knife. Do not overcook the potatoes. Remove the potatoes and cool. Discard the carrots.

③ Peel the potatoes, slice into ¼-inch rounds, and place them in a large bowl.

④ Add the cumin, onion, preserved lemon rind, olives, fennel, lemon juice, and olive oil. Toss to combine. Adjust the seasoning with salt and pepper. Garnish with chopped fennel fronds.

SIMPLE GRITS

MAKES 6 SERVINGS

While I might be known as a chef who relishes fancy food and international ingredients, I love plenty of good old American foods as well. Grits are a special favorite of mine. They have a wonderful texture and what goes better with gravy than grits? I serve these creamy grits with Garlicky Pot Roast (page 68) and Falling-off-the-Bone Short Ribs (page 88). You can also use water to make a pareve version.

8 cups Essential Chicken Stock (page 207) or water

Olive oil

2 cups regular grits (not quick-cooking or instant)

½ cup chopped fresh flat-leaf parsley

½ cup chopped scallions, white and green parts (about 8 scallions)

Kosher salt and freshly ground black pepper

① Place the chicken stock in a large saucepan and bring to a boil.

② Lightly coat a slow cooker insert with olive oil (this helps keep the grits from sticking). Preheat the slow cooker to High. Add the grits and stock to the insert and stir to combine. Cook on High for 6 hours, until thick and tender (the texture should be sort of soft, not too gritty).

③ Stir in the parsley and scallions and adjust the seasoning with salt and pepper. Serve hot or warm.

CHEESY GRITS

DAIRY

Serve these creamy grits with Braised Eggs in Spicy Tomato Sauce (page 134) for a delicious brunch. You can get everything started before you go to bed and wake up to your breakfast already made. So efficient—just pour the coffee and you are ready to go.

8 cups water

2 cups regular grits (not quick-cooking or instant)

Kosher salt and freshly ground black pepper

Olive oil

½ cup chopped fresh flat-leaf parsley

½ cup chopped scallions, white and green parts (about 8 scallions)

2 cups grated sharp Cheddar cheese (½ pound)

1. Place the water in a large pot and bring to a boil. Add the grits and add a dash each of salt and pepper.
2. Lightly coat a slow cooker insert with olive oil (this helps keep the grits from sticking). Preheat the slow cooker to High.
3. Pour the grits and water into the slow cooker insert. Cook on High for 6 hours, until thick and tender (the texture should be sort of soft, not too gritty).
4. Turn the machine to Low or Warm (if the cooker has that setting). Stir in the parsley, scallions, and cheese. The hot grits will melt the cheese.
5. Adjust the seasoning with salt and pepper, and serve when you are ready.

CARROTS WITH DRIED CURRANTS

PAREVE

MAKES 5 SERVINGS

This carrot salad can be made up to 2 days ahead of serving and stored, covered, in the refrigerator. It is not made in a slow cooker but I serve it as a side dish with Lamb Tagine (page 104). The bright color and refreshing flavor of this salad complement the richness of the lamb tagine as part of a Moroccan feast. I love the unexpected sweetness of the dried currants contrasting with the earthy cumin.

6 medium carrots, peeled and grated on the coarse side of a box grater

½ cup dried currants

Grated zest and juice of 1 orange (see Note)

½ teaspoon toasted cumin seeds (see page 199), ground

3 tablespoons extra-virgin olive oil

¼ cup chopped fresh mint leaves

Kosher salt and freshly ground black pepper

1. Place the grated carrots in a clean towel. Squeeze out the excess carrot juice. (Otherwise the juice would pool in the bottom of the salad and make it soggy.)
2. In a large bowl, toss together the carrots, currants, orange zest and juice, cumin, olive oil, and mint. Adjust the seasoning with salt and pepper.

NOTE

▶ First grate the zest with a Microplane, then cut the fruit in half and squeeze the juice.

CREAMY COLESLAW

MAKES 8 CUPS

PAREVE

I make this slaw when I am looking for a quick, refreshing side dish. The combination of creamy aïoli and crunchy cabbage makes it an ideal topper for sandwiches made from Rubbed Brisket (page 64). I like slaw to be a little spicy, but you can leave out the harissa if you prefer a milder version.

The coleslaw can be stored, covered, in the refrigerator for to 3 days.

1 small head red cabbage (about 1½ pounds)

1 small red onion, very thinly sliced

2 medium carrots, peeled and grated on the coarse side of a box grater

½ cup Homemade Aïoli (page 185), Herbed Aïoli Dipping Sauce (page 186), or store-bought mayonnaise

2 tablespoons sugar

Grated zest and juice of 1 lime (see Note, page 148)

2 teaspoons Harissa (page 181; optional)

Kosher salt and freshly ground black pepper

1. Remove the outer leaves of the cabbage and discard; the outer leaves tend to be dry and bruised. Cut the cabbage in quarters from the root end to the top. Cut out the core from each quarter and discard. Lay the cabbage cut side down and cut very thin cross sections.

2. Place the cabbage, onion, and carrots in a large bowl. Combine the aïoli, sugar, lime zest and juice, and harissa (if using) in a small bowl. Add to the vegetables and toss to coat them completely. Adjust the seasoning with salt and pepper.

LEMON RISOTTO

DAIRY

MAKES 6 SIDE SERVINGS OR 4
MAIN-COURSE SERVINGS

This decadent version of the Italian classic makes a perfect side dish or first course. I like to serve it garnished with shards of Parmesan cheese. The tangy lemon and salty cheese combine to create a big WOW flavor, and the mascarpone cheese puts this creamy, decadent dish over the top.

Olive oil

2 large shallots, finely minced

1 garlic clove, finely minced

2 cups Arborio rice

½ cup dry white wine such as chardonnay

Grated zest and juice of 1 large lemon
    (see Note)

2½ cups Vegetable Stock (page 211)

3 tablespoons mascarpone cheese

¼ cup chopped fresh flat-leaf parsley

1 tablespoon chopped fresh thyme

Kosher salt and freshly ground black
    pepper

SUGGESTED GARNISHES

Parmesan cheese, preferably Parmigiano-Reggiano, shaved into large shards with a vegetable peeler

1. Place a medium sauté pan over medium heat. Lightly coat the bottom of the pan with olive oil. Add the shallots and cook until soft and translucent but not colored. Add the garlic and cook for 3 minutes more. Add the rice and stir until the rice grains are coated with oil.

2. Add the wine and increase the heat to medium-high. Bring to a simmer. Transfer the mixture to a slow cooker insert. Stir in the lemon zest and juice and the stock. Cover and cook on High for 2 hours, until the rice is cooked through and creamy but still slightly firm or resistant when tasted.

3. Stir in the mascarpone cheese, parsley, and thyme. Season to taste with salt and pepper.

4. Place the risotto on a large platter or in individual bowls and garnish with Parmesan cheese. Serve immediately.

NOTE

▶ First grate the zest with a Microplane, then cut the lemon in half and squeeze the juice.

VARIATION

Add 2 cups sliced cooked asparagus or any other favorite vegetable.

HERBED QUINOA PILAF

MAKES 6 TO 8 SERVINGS

My kids make fun of me when Passover approaches. They know that they will be eating this quinoa (a seed, not a grain) many times throughout the holiday. I use the tasty little bead other times during the year, but I guess it has become cliché to see boxes of the stuff lined up before the holiday begins.

I love this relative newcomer to many menus. Many rabbinical authorities have given quinoa their blessing for use during the "grain-less" holiday. I use quinoa as a side dish, salad embellishment, soup addition, and as a main dish with the addition of ground poultry or meat. Made with vegetable stock or water, it can be served with any type of meal.

The quinoa can be stored, covered, in the refrigerator for up to 3 days or frozen for up to 1 month. To reheat gently, preheat the oven to 300°F. Place the quinoa in a casserole, add a little stock or water, and cover. Reheat in the oven for 15 to 20 minutes.

2 cups quinoa

4 cups Essential Chicken Stock (page 207), Vegetable Stock (page 211), or water

¼ cup chopped flat-leaf parsley

1 tablespoon chopped fresh thyme

¼ cup toasted pine nuts (see page 199)

½ cup golden raisins

Kosher salt and freshly ground black pepper

MEAT or Pareve

1. Place the quinoa in a large bowl filled with cold water. Rub the grains between your hands to remove the natural saponins that can give the quinoa a bitter taste. Pour the quinoa into a fine-mesh sieve to drain the water and rinse briefly under running water. The quinoa is now ready to be cooked.

2. Place the quinoa in the slow cooker insert. Add the chicken stock, cover, and cook on Low for 4 hours.

3. Drain the quinoa, straining out any unabsorbed liquid. Place the quinoa in a large bowl. Stir in the parsley, thyme, pine nuts, and raisins. Season to taste with salt and pepper. Serve immediately.

MOROCCAN-SPICED
MIXED GRAIN "RISOTTO"

MEAT or Pareve

MAKES 10 SERVINGS

An authentic risotto uses Arborio or Carnaroli, another short-grain rice from Italy. This fragrant version uses several whole grains including quinoa and purple sticky rice, cooked slowly to allow their natural starchiness to create a creamy, comforting dish. The quinoa in this dish adds a complete protein, so you can serve it as an entrée as well as a side. If you can't find all the grains, feel free to experiment with different grains or just omit some of them. Each addition you make will add a new element to the dish. And making it pareve with water allows you to serve it with anything.

The mixed grain risotto can be stored, covered, in the refrigerator for up to 3 days. It can also be frozen for up to 2 months. To reheat gently, preheat the oven to 300°F. Place the risotto in a casserole, add a little stock or water, and cover. Reheat in the oven for 15 to 20 minutes.

Olive oil

1 large Spanish onion, diced

3 garlic cloves, minced

2 tablespoons tomato paste

2 tablespoons Moroccan Spice Mix (page 201)

3 tablespoons fresh lemon juice

½ cup dry white wine (I prefer chardonnay)

½ cup farro (see Notes; see Sources, page 233)

½ cup dried chick peas, sorted through, soaked overnight, and drained

½ cup black beluga lentils (see Notes; see Sources, page 233)

1 cup purple sticky rice (see Notes; see Sources, page 233)

1 cup black or regular quinoa (see Notes; see Sources, page 233)

5 cups Essential Chicken Stock (page 207) or water

1 cup golden raisins

Kosher salt and freshly ground black pepper

1. Preheat a slow cooker insert to High. Place a large sauté pan over medium heat. Lightly coat the bottom of the pan with olive oil. Cook the onion until softened and translucent but not colored, about 10 minutes. Add the garlic and cook for 2 minutes more. Turn up the heat to medium-high and add the tomato paste and spice mix. Stir until combined thoroughly. Add the lemon juice and wine. Cook for 3 minutes more.

2. Transfer the onion mixture to the slow cooker. Add the farro, chick peas, lentils, sticky rice, quinoa, and stock and stir thoroughly. Cover and cook on High for 3 hours, until all the liquid is absorbed and the chick peas are tender.

3. Add the raisins and salt and pepper to taste. Serve immediately, or turn the cooker to Low or Warm (if the cooker has that setting), and keep warm until you are ready to serve.

NOTES

▶ Purple sticky rice is a glutinous rice from Asia. While the rice does not contain dietary gluten, it becomes sticky or glue-like in texture when cooked. Purple rice gets its color from the natural outer layer called the bran, which has not been removed. Purple rice is gorgeous and has a nutty flavor. It can be found in many specialty markets, grocery stores, and online (see Sources, page 233).

▶ Black beluga lentils are descriptively named after their resemblance to beluga caviar. They are very tiny and hold their shape even when cooked for a long time.

▶ I recently discovered black quinoa. The "bead" of black quinoa is much smaller than regular quinoa. It also has a bit of a stronger flavor.

▶ I fell in love with farro several years ago. The grain resembles a large grain of barley. Farro tastes nutty and holds its shape well when cooked in the slow cooker. Farro is grown exclusively in Italy, where it is highly prized.

KASHA VARNISHKES

MEAT
or Pareve

MAKES 5 SERVINGS

This European comfort food makes a delicious side dish. The buckwheat groats—"kasha" to many—are nutty and have a toothsome texture. I like to serve this on Shabbat with some chopped-up huevos haminados *(Stewed Eggs, page 156) added. The two dishes may be from different parts of the world, but they will act like old friends on your plate and your taste buds. Together the two side dishes make one satisfying main dish.*

Serve this savory pasta dish warm with Rubbed Brisket (page 64). Make it pareve with olive oil and water, and you can follow it with a dairy dessert.

2 tablespoons chicken fat, duck fat, or olive oil

1 large Spanish onion, diced

1 cup uncooked bow tie pasta

1 cup medium buckwheat groats (kasha)

1 large egg, beaten

2 cups Essential Chicken Stock (page 207) or water

Kosher salt and freshly ground black pepper

① Place a medium saucepan over medium heat. Lightly coat the bottom of the pan with fat. Cook the onion in the pan until it is soft and translucent but not colored. Transfer the onion to a slow cooker insert.

② Add the bow tie pasta to the saucepan. Toast the pasta for several minutes, stirring, until it is lightly browned. Transfer the pasta to the insert.

③ In a small bowl, stir together the groats and the egg. Make sure the groats are completed coated with the egg.

④ Add a little more fat to the saucepan and add the groats. Stir the groats until the egg begins to set and cook, about 3 minutes. Transfer the mixture to the slow cooker. Add the chicken stock. Cover and cook on Low for 90 minutes or until all of the liquid has been absorbed.

⑤ Add salt and pepper to taste and serve immediately.

MASHED SWEET POTATOES

MEAT
or Pareve

MAKES 6 TO 8 SERVINGS

Sweet potatoes made in the slow cooker are the way to go. I don't have to fuss, and the potatoes are delicious and creamy every time. I also use my slow cooker to help keep mashed potatoes warm during a holiday dinner like Thanksgiving. I place two piles of mashed potatoes in the insert, one russet and one sweet, and keep the machine at a Low setting, which holds the potatoes at a perfect temperature until I'm ready to serve them. The potatoes will hold for up to 3 hours.

The potatoes can be served by themselves or spooned on top of Shepherd's Pie (page 95) for a delicious, creamy crust. Use vegetable stock or water for a pareve version.

4 large sweet potatoes (about 4 pounds), preferably garnet, peeled and cut into medium cubes

2 medium carrots, peeled and diced

2 large Granny Smith apples, peeled, cored, and cut into large dice

1 cup warm Essential Chicken Stock (page 207), Vegetable Stock (page 211), or water plus ¼ cup additional liquid for mashing

1 tablespoon Ancho Chile Powder (optional; page 200, or see Sources, page 233)

Kosher salt and freshly ground black pepper

1. Preheat a slow cooker to High. Place the sweet potatoes, carrots, apples, and 1 cup of stock in the slow cooker insert. Cover and cook on High for 3 hours, until the potatoes are very soft and falling apart.

2. Mash the mixture with a potato masher or put through a ricer. If the potatoes are too thick, stir in more liquid a spoonful at a time.

3. Add the ancho chile powder, if using, and salt and pepper to taste.

STEWED EGGS

PAREVE

MAKES 8 EGGS

I have been enjoying these creamy, toffee-colored eggs—called huevos haminados *in Spanish—for years. I use the eggs for my seders and Passover lunches. They are a delicious side dish for Shabbat meals. Chopped and mixed with Homemade Aïoli (page 185), they make a great egg salad.*

Skins from 1 dozen yellow onions (brown skins)

8 large eggs

1 tablespoon olive oil

2 tablespoons coffee grounds or instant coffee

1 teaspoon kosher salt

1 teaspoon freshly ground black pepper

1 Place the onion skins in the bottom of a slow cooker insert. Nestle the eggs in the onion skins.

2 Drizzle the olive oil on top of the eggs. Scatter the coffee over the eggs. Sprinkle with the salt and pepper and add water to just cover.

3 Cover and cook on Low for at least 10 hours.

4 Wipe off the eggs and serve either warm or chilled.

CANDIED KUMQUATS

MAKES ABOUT 4 CUPS

PAREVE

Just when you think that there is nothing fun to eat in the middle of winter, kumquats appear in the market. These charming little citrus fruits look and taste like miniature oval oranges. My kids actually think they taste brighter and more "orangey" than their plus-sized cousins.

I make a big batch of candied kumquats once or twice a season and store them in the refrigerator. They keep for up to 3 months. The cooker does all the work and I get the rewards. I serve kumquats as garnishes for salads and fruit compotes, and as a gorgeous addition to Moroccan-Spiced Duck (page 120). I like to add peppercorns for a bit of "bite" and balance, but you can leave them out for a more straightforward sweet dish.

2 cups sugar

2 cups water

One 2- to 3-inch cinnamon stick

1 tablespoon whole cloves

2 teaspoons whole black peppercorns

3 pieces whole star anise

2 pounds kumquats (about 30)

1. Preheat a slow cooker to High. Place the sugar and water in a large saucepan and bring to a boil. Turn the heat down and simmer for 5 minutes. Transfer the syrup to the slow cooker insert. Add the cinnamon stick, cloves, peppercorns, star anise, and kumquats. Cover and cook on High for 90 minutes.

2. Transfer to a storage container and cool completely.

3. Store the kumquats in the refrigerator in the flavored syrup, covered, for up to 3 months.

Desserts
and Breakfast

I feel a recipe is only a theme, which an
intelligent cook can play each time with a variation.
—MADAME BENOIT

We love dessert in our house and especially enjoy *baking together—when there is time.* When time is short, however, dessert or special or hearty breakfasts are often knocked off the menu.

With the slow cooker at the ready, there is no need to skip dessert. I can poach fruit to perfection with minimal effort, loading up on my favorites at the farmers' market and jazzing up a classic Peach Melba (page 165) with a ripe Raspberry Coulis (page 193) or a quick Sparkling Sabayon (page 192). I can also take advantage of the elusively ripe pear. Pears always seem either too hard or too soft, but after a nice long dunk in the slow cooker, Poached Pears (page 172) are ready to eat with a simple drizzle of chocolate sauce or pomegranate molasses. With the slow cooker in action, Friday night's dessert can be on its way by Friday morning.

I am a professional chef who still has spent my fair share of time covering up the cracks that inevitably form on my cheesecakes. The slow cooker solves that problem entirely. The gentle constant temperature prevents the cracks, resulting in a velvety-textured and smooth cheesecake. I simply throw the batter together for my family's favorite Key Lime Cheesecake (page 168) and head out the door. By the time I get home the cheesecake needs a bit of a chill in the refrigerator and we are ready to eat.

I am also a flan fanatic. I just cannot get enough of this luxuriously simple dessert. While flan is a snap to assemble, normally it has to be watched throughout its long cook time to ensure it is not overcooked. My version of slow-cooked Flan (page 166) has the same texture and flavor of its traditional cousin, without waiting for a timer to go off.

When it comes to breakfast, I feel like an absolute genius when I wake up to the smell of Maple-Pecan Bread Pudding (page 176) ready and waiting for me. I push the button on the coffee pot and I am ready to go. The best part is, I get to spend more time sleeping or with my kids. If you have never thought of making oatmeal in the slow cooker and have settled for quick-cooking oats or microwaved oatmeal, you owe it yourself to try the fabulously chewy and nutty steel-cut oats, the healthier and more interesting cousin to rolled oats. I simply prepare a couple of quick toppings for everyone to customize their own bowl and we're all happy.

My secret to cooking great desserts or breakfasts in the slow cooker is to keep things simple. There is no need to attempt lavish, complicated recipes. Just go for the straightforward recipes filled with real, wholesome ingredients and you can eat well from breakfast to dessert, every day of the week.

BLACK FOREST BREAD PUDDING

DAIRY

MAKES 4 SERVINGS,
OR 1 JUST FOR JONAH!

This luscious version of bread pudding is a winter favorite. As my son Jonah says, "It has all the food groups in it: chocolate, chocolate, and chocolate." It is great hot or chilled.

Allow it to cool completely and store, covered, in the refrigerator for up to 3 days.

1 tablespoon unsalted butter, melted,
    plus extra for greasing the insert
2 cups half-and-half
1 cup whole milk
½ cup unsweetened cocoa powder,
    preferably Valrhona
4 large eggs
1 cup tightly packed light brown sugar
½ cup granulated sugar
¼ cup Kirsch
Seeds scraped from 1 split vanilla bean,
    or 2 teaspoons vanilla extract
Ten 1½-inch-thick slices day-old bread
½ cup dried cherries, preferably sour
1 cup frozen cherries, sliced in half and
    pitted (see Note)
½ cup bittersweet chocolate, preferably
    Callebaut, cut into medium-sized
    chunks

½ cup white chocolate, preferably
    Callebaut, cut into medium-sized
    chunks

SUGGESTED GARNISHES
Freshly whipped cream

1. Lightly grease a 6½-quart slow cooker insert. In a large bowl, whisk together the half-and-half, milk, and cocoa powder until thoroughly combined. Whisk in the eggs, melted butter, sugars, Kirsch, and vanilla.
2. Layer the bread in the insert. Scatter the dried and frozen cherries evenly over the bread. Sprinkle the chocolate chunks over the cherries. Pour the custard over the bread. Cover and cook on High for 3 hours, or until the custard has been cooked through and the bread is no longer soggy and has firmed up slightly.
3. Scoop the bread pudding into dessert glasses and serve with freshly whipped cream.

NOTE
▶ I love using sour frozen cherries, but sweet will be delicious here as well.

CHOCOLATE–ANCHO CHILE PUDDING CAKE WITH SPARKLING SABAYON

PAREVE

MAKES 6 SERVINGS

You will never be able to say you didn't have time to make dessert when you taste how luxuriously rich and deeply flavored this cake is and see how easy the recipe is in the slow cooker. The slow cooker makes baking a snap. This warm comforting cake has all the ingredients to make it a top-notch dessert. Don't hold back on using the best chocolate and vanilla possible. With so few ingredients in a dish, it is important that each one be of the highest quality.

You will need a rack to support the soufflé dish in which the cake bakes. If you do not have a rack, roll a large piece of foil into a long, thick rope. Bring the ends together to form a ring that will support the soufflé dish, with a bit of space all around it. You want the heat to circulate evenly around the dish.

If the idea of a spicy dessert is too unusual, you can leave out the ancho chile powder and the dessert will still be fabulous; but do try the spicy version sometime.

Canola oil

3 ounces bittersweet chocolate, preferably Callebaut, chopped

1 tablespoon vanilla extract

3 tablespoons brewed coffee or water

1 tablespoon espresso powder

1 tablespoon Ancho Chile Powder (page 200, or see Sources, page 233)

1 cup all-purpose flour

¼ cup unsweetened cocoa powder, preferably Valrhona

2 teaspoons baking powder

Pinch of kosher salt

¾ cup sugar

2 large eggs

Sparkling Sabayon (page 192)

1. Lightly grease a 3-quart soufflé dish with canola oil. Insert a rack or foil ring in a slow cooker insert large enough to hold the soufflé dish.

2. Bring a medium saucepan of water to a boil. Place a heatproof bowl over the pan so the bottom of the bowl does not touch the water. Stir together the chocolate, vanilla, coffee, espresso powder, and ancho chile powder in the bowl until smooth. Remove from the heat and allow the mixture to cool completely.

3. In a medium bowl, stir together the flour, cocoa powder, baking powder, and salt.

4. Whip the sugar and eggs with an electric mixer at high speed 3 to 5 minutes, until a ribbon forms when the beater is lifted and the egg mixture holds the ribbon on top of the surface. Gently fold the chocolate mixture into the egg mixture, being careful not to deflate the eggs. Fold in the flour mixture. Pour the batter into the prepared soufflé dish. Cover and cook on High for 3 hours.

5. Allow the cake to stand at room temperature for 30 minutes before serving. Scoop into dessert glasses and drizzle Sparkling Sabayon over and around each serving.

WILD RICE PUDDING

MAKES 6 TO 8 SERVINGS

I was inspired by this dish after reading a book about how Chicago, my hometown, used to have wild rice growing along the banks of the Chicago River. The Native Americans treasured the harvest and used the ingredient in many dishes. Sadly, this native plant no longer grows locally, but we can still enjoy it for breakfast.

1 cup wild rice

1½ cups short-grain brown rice

½ cup tightly packed light brown sugar

½ cup granulated sugar

¼ cup dried cranberries

¼ cup dried blueberries

Seeds scraped from ½ split vanilla bean
    or 2 teaspoons vanilla extract

2 teaspoons ground cinnamon

Grated zest and juice of 1 orange
    (see Note)

2 tablespoons (¼ stick) unsalted
    butter, melted

3 cups milk, preferably whole

1 cup heavy cream

SUGGESTED GARNISHES

Maple syrup or honey, heavy cream or half-and-half

1. Stir together the wild rice, brown rice, sugars, dried fruit, vanilla, cinnamon, orange zest and juice, melted butter, milk, and cream in a slow cooker insert. Cover and cook on Low for 4 hours or until all the liquid is absorbed and the rices are tender.

2. Serve with a drizzle of maple syrup or honey and additional cream.

NOTE

▶ First grate the zest with a Microplane, then cut the orange in half and squeeze the juice.

PEACH MELBA

As much I love peaches, it is hard to find the fruit at its perfect eating-out-of-hand ripeness. The slow cooker takes fresh peaches and slowly poaches them to the perfect tender, juicy texture that makes the fruit one of my favorites. Shop for the seasonal fruit as they will be the most flavorful and delicious. I like to poach a large batch and store them in the refrigerator in the poaching liquid for up to 5 days.

Just like the original, I generously top the peaches with crimson, tart raspberry sauce. If you want to keep it classic—and dairy—serve the peaches and coulis over ice cream. To keep it pareve, substitute the Sparkling Sabayon.

The peaches can be stored in their poaching liquid for up to 3 days, covered, in the refrigerator. The poaching liquid can also be used to poach more peaches. Store the liquid in the refrigerator for up to 3 weeks.

2 cups sugar

1 cup water

1 cup sweet white wine such as Moscato or Riesling

1 vanilla bean, split lengthwise but not scraped

PAREVE or Dairy

3 firm but ripe peaches

1 cup Raspberry Coulis (page 193)

1 cup Sparkling Sabayon (page 192; optional)

SUGGESTED GARNISHES

Chopped toasted hazelnuts (see page 199), fresh mint, fresh raspberries, whipped cream, vanilla ice cream

1. Preheat a 6½-quart slow cooker to Low. Combine the sugar, water, and wine in a medium saucepan over medium-high heat. Bring to a simmer and cook for 5 minutes. Transfer the syrup to the slow cooker insert. Add the vanilla bean and peaches. Cover and cook on Low for 3 hours.

2. Gently remove the peaches from the slow cooker and allow them to cool down. Reserve the poaching liquid. Split the peaches in half. Pull out the pit and slide off the skins.

3. Serve the peach halves in dessert bowls or sliced in wineglasses, drizzled with the Raspberry Coulis and the Sparkling Sabayon, if using, and topped with your choice of garnish.

FLAN

DAIRY

MAKES 8 SERVINGS

This flan gets its addictively sensuous texture from the decadent mixture of eggs and sweet evaporated milk cooked in the slow cooker. I use a 5-inch round cake pan with 4-inch-high sides (most often used for wedding cake tops) that fits into my slow cooker. If you cannot find the wedding cake pan, I recommend using an 8 × 4–inch loaf pan and serving the flan in slices. I used a loaf pan for a large Shavuot party and kept the flans baking around the clock. The flan can be stored in the refrigerator, covered, for up to 3 days.

You'll find it easier to use a candy thermometer for this recipe than to rely just on the appearance of the caramel. You will need a rack to support the pan in which the flan bakes at least 1 inch off the bottom of the insert. If you do not have a rack, roll a large piece of foil into a long, thick rope. Bring the ends together to form a ring that will support the pan, with a bit of space all around it.

1½ cups sugar

5 large eggs

One 12-ounce can evaporated milk (not nonfat)

One 14-ounce can sweetened condensed milk (not nonfat)

Seeds scraped from 1 split vanilla bean or 2 teaspoons vanilla extract

1. Preheat a 6½-quart slow cooker to High.
2. Place 1 cup of the sugar in a small saucepan over medium-high heat. Cook the sugar until it has completely liquefied and turned a dark caramel color or registers 350°F on a candy thermometer. Do not walk away, as this happens fairly quickly.
3. Pour the caramel into the flan pan. Tilt the pan so that the caramel covers the bottom of the pan completely. Set the pan aside to cool.
4. In a large bowl, thoroughly whisk together the remaining ½ cup sugar, the eggs, evaporated milk, condensed milk, and vanilla. Pour the mixture into the flan pan.

⑤ Place the flan pan into the slow cooker on top of the rack. Place several layers of paper towels over the top of the flan pan. The paper towels should not touch the flan. (This will keep any condensation off the flan.) Cover and cook on High for 2½ hours. Allow the flan to cool in the slow cooker for another 2 hours before uncovering.

⑥ Remove the pan from the insert and chill the flan for 4 hours.

⑦ Run a knife around the sides of the pan. Hold a serving plate on top of the flan and invert the pan. The flan should drop gently out of the pan and onto the plate. If it does not drop out of the pan, repeat the process. Drizzle the caramel sauce from the flan pan over the dessert.

KEY LIME CHEESECAKE

DAIRY

MAKES 8 SERVINGS

My son Ari loves this tart vanilla-infused cheesecake. My slow cooker–baked cheese-cakes never crack, and they always have the most incredible velvety texture.

You will need a rack to support the pan in which the cheesecake bakes at least 1 inch off the bottom of the insert. If you do not have a rack, roll a large piece of foil into a long, thick rope. Bring the ends together to form a ring that will support the pan, with a bit of space all around it.

The cheesecake can be made 2 days ahead of serving and stored in the springform pan, covered, in the refrigerator.

FOR THE LIME CUSTARD

- 6 large egg yolks
- ¾ cup sugar
- 2 teaspoons vanilla extract
- 6 tablespoons fresh or bottled Key lime juice or fresh regular lime juice
- 1 teaspoon grated Key lime or regular lime zest

FOR THE CRUST

- 8 tablespoons (1 stick) unsalted butter, melted, plus extra for the pan
- 1¾ cups graham cracker crumbs (about 12 whole graham crackers)
- 3 tablespoons sugar
- ½ teaspoon kosher salt

FOR THE FILLING

- Two 8-ounce packages cream cheese, at room temperature
- ⅔ cup sugar
- 2 large eggs
- 2 teaspoons vanilla extract
- 3 tablespoons fresh or bottled Key lime juice
- 1 tablespoon grated Key lime or regular lime zest

SUGGESTED GARNISHES

Fresh lime slices

1. **Make the Lime Custard.** Combine the egg yolks, sugar, vanilla, lime juice, and lime zest in a small heavy saucepan. Whisk over medium heat until the custard thickens, about 8 minutes, then simmer for 30 seconds more. Remove from the heat. Cool to room temperature, stirring occasionally. The mixture will thicken further while cooling.

2. **Make the Crust.** Wrap foil around the outside of a 7-inch springform pan with 3-inch sides.

3. Lightly butter the springform pan. Stir together the graham cracker crumbs, sugar, and salt in a medium bowl. Mix in the melted butter until completely moistened. Press the crumb mixture evenly onto the bottom and 1½ inches up the sides of the pan.

4. **Make the Filling.** Place the cream cheese, sugar, the eggs, vanilla, lime juice, and lime zest in a food processor. Process until the ingredients are completely mixed.

5. **Assemble and Bake the Cake.** Spoon the lime custard into the crust. Smooth the top. Carefully spoon the filling over the custard and distribute evenly.

6. Place the pan in a 6½-quart slow cooker insert on top of a rack. Place several layers of paper towels over the springform pan. The paper towels should not touch the cake. (This will keep any condensation off the cake.)

7. Cover and cook on High for 2½ hours. Do not lift the cover, as heat will escape and change the cook time.

8. Allow the cheesecake to remain in the turned-off slow cooker for at least 2 hours after the cook time is over.

9. Remove the springform pan from the insert and chill the cheesecake for at least 4 hours or overnight.

10. Slide a knife around the outside edge of the cheesecake. Loosen the clip on the pan and separate the collar from the bottom. Leave the cake on the base of the pan to cut. Garnish with fresh lime slices.

PERSIMMON PUDDING

DAIRY
or Pareve

MAKES 8 SERVINGS

Versions of this classic Native American dish often hail from the Midwest, where persimmons flourish in the cool fall. This dish tastes similar to pumpkin pie but is very dark in color. I am not a fan of pareve pumpkin pie, but often crave the flavor and spices of that classic autumnal favorite. Persimmon pudding has the texture and flavors that I can't get enough of when the weather turns cool. The slow cooker makes the long cooking process a "piece of cake." I just whir the ingredients together and let the machine take over. I like to spoon the hot pudding into dessert glasses and garnish it with Sparkling Sabayon for a pareve dessert or whipped cream for a dairy treat. Persimmon pudding is warm and comforting hot but equally delicious cold.

Persimmons are grown throughout the United States and Asia and come in two basic varieties, astringent and nonastringent. The astringent Hachiya variety needs to be fully ripened before eating or it is unpalatable. A ripe persimmon will be bright orange in color and very soft. Look for Fuyu persimmons,

which appear in the markets usually in the late fall. Or, if you are lucky enough to be in the Midwest during that time, you can often find persimmons in farmers' markets.

The pudding can be stored in a covered container in the refrigerator for up to 3 days.

6 to 8 fully ripe persimmons

Canola oil

3 cups whole milk or soy milk

2 cups sugar

3 large eggs

2 cups all-purpose flour

1 teaspoon baking powder

1 teaspoon baking soda

2 teaspoons vanilla extract

2 teaspoons ground cinnamon

½ teaspoon freshly grated nutmeg

SUGGESTED GARNISHES
Sparkling Sabayon (page 192), whipped cream

1. Process the persimmons in a food processor until they are completely pureed. Strain the puree through a fine-mesh strainer to remove the skin and seeds. (It should make 2 cups of puree.)

2. Lightly grease a 3-quart soufflé dish with canola oil. Place the empty soufflé dish into a 6½-quart slow cooker insert. Add enough hot water to the insert so that it comes about halfway up the sides of the soufflé dish. Remove the soufflé dish. Preheat the slow cooker to High.

3. Place the persimmon puree, milk, sugar, eggs, flour, baking powder, baking soda, vanilla, cinnamon, and nutmeg in the bowl of a stand mixer. Using the paddle attachment, mix until everything is just combined. Do not overmix. I usually finish mixing this by hand so as not to activate the gluten in the flour, which can make a dessert rubbery or tough.

4. Pour the batter into the prepared soufflé dish. Place the soufflé dish into the water bath. Cover and cook on High for 3 to 4 hours, until a toothpick inserted comes out clean.

5. Spoon the pudding into dessert glasses or bowls. Serve with Sparkling Sabayon or whipped cream.

POACHED PEARS
WITH SWEET MASCARPONE

DAIRY
or Pareve

MAKES 8 SERVINGS

Pears are absolutely my favorite fruit. They are elegant in shape, beautifully perfumed, and versatile enough to be a stand-alone dessert or a fabulous follow-up to cheese or poultry. The only problem with pears is that they go from too hard to overripe in what seems to be minutes. It is difficult to capture them in that perfect stage of ultimate "pearness." That is where poached pears come in. If you poach slightly underripe pears in red wine, they take on this gorgeous garnet color, look incredibly dressy, and have an amazing succulent texture. You can top them simply or elaborately.

The pears hold up for days at a time and can be served at your leisure. They can be made up to 5 days before serving and stored in the poaching liquid, covered, in the refrigerator. Once the pears are gone, the poaching liquid can be stored, covered, in the refrigerator for up to 3 weeks, and used again to poach more pears. Or reduce the poaching liquid to make a syrup for serving the pears.

If you are serving this after a meat meal, omit the mascarpone filling, of course. The pears will still be luscious.

FOR THE PEARS

1 bottle (750 ml) dry red wine such as pinot noir or cabernet sauvignon

One 2- to 3-inch cinnamon stick

1 whole star anise

6 whole black peppercorns (about ¼ teaspoon)

1 cup tightly packed light brown sugar

1 cup granulated sugar

1 bay leaf

8 small firm pears such as forelle or Bartlett

FOR THE SWEET MASCARPONE

½ cup mascarpone cheese, at room temperature

1 teaspoon vanilla extract

2 teaspoons heavy cream

¼ cup granulated sugar

Chopped unsalted pistachios (optional)

Sparkling Sabayon (page 192), reduced poaching liquid, pomegranate molasses, chocolate sauce, chopped pistachios

1. **Make the Pears.** Preheat a 6½-quart slow cooker to High.

2. Combine the wine, cinnamon stick, star anise, peppercorns, sugars, and bay leaf in the slow cooker insert. Whisk together to help dissolve the sugar.

3. Peel the pears straight down, from the stem end to the flower end, to give a uniform appearance. Place the pears immediately into the poaching liquid.

4. Cut a piece of parchment paper that will fit into the slow cooker and cover the surface of the pears. Weight down the parchment lightly with an empty pie plate. This keeps the pears down in the poaching liquid as they are quite buoyant.

5. Cover and cook on High for 4 hours, or until a paring knife easily pierces a pear. Remove the pears with a slotted spoon and cool completely. To serve the pears with the filling, cut the pears lengthwise. Using a melon baller, scoop out the core and discard.

6. Strain and reserve the poaching liquid to use again, or strain it into a medium saucepan and simmer over high heat until it reduces to a syrup to drizzle over the pears.

7. **Make the Sweet Mascarpone.** Whisk together the mascarpone, vanilla, cream, sugar, and pistachios (if using) in a small bowl.

8. Dollop the mascarpone filling on top of the hollowed-out pears.

9. Serve the pears with the reduced poaching liquid, if using, and your choice of garnish.

POACHED FRUIT COMPOTE

PAREVE or Dairy

MAKES 8 SERVINGS

While some swear that eating fresh fruit is the only way to enjoy this delicious seasonal treasure, many fruits definitely benefit from a nice long poach in a fragrant liquid. It is not always easy to find fruit in the perfect stage of ripeness, but when slightly underripe fruit are slow cooked, they soften and become juicy and delicately flavored. I wrote this recipe with the combination of peaches, apples, and plums, but there are no rules regarding which fruits to use. I do recommend that you choose firm, slightly underripe fruits as they will hold up better to the long, slow poach. I served this gorgeous colorful dessert for Sukkot. It was a true celebration of the season and bounty of fruit.

This delicious compote can be served warm with ice cream or Sparkling Sabayon (page 192), or topped with yogurt and granola for a scrumptious breakfast or snack. It is equally delicious cold.

The compote can be stored, covered, in the refrigerator for up to 1 week, or frozen for up to 1 month. Once the fruit is gone, the poaching liquid can be stored, covered, in the refrigerator for up to 3 weeks, and used again to poach more fruit.

3 large peaches (firm, with no bruises)

2 large apples such as Honeycrisp (firm, with no bruises)

2 large plums (firm, with no bruises; see Notes)

2 cups sugar

1 bottle (750 ml) sweet white wine such as Moscato

1 large rosemary sprigs

6 whole black peppercorns (about ¼ teaspoon)

Grated zest and juice of 1 lemon (see Notes)

SUGGESTED GARNISHES

Raspberry Coulis (page 193), Sparkling Sabayon (page 192), vanilla ice cream, yogurt, granola

1. Preheat a slow cooker to High.
2. Combine the peaches, apples, plums, sugar, wine, rosemary, peppercorns, and lemon zest and juice in the slow cooker insert. Stir to help dissolve the sugar.
3. Cut a piece of parchment paper that will fit into the slow cooker and cover the surface of the fruits. Weight down the parchment lightly with an empty pie plate. This keeps the fruits down in the poaching liquid as they are quite buoyant.
4. Cover and cook on High for 2 hours.
5. Remove the fruits gently with a slotted spoon and set aside to cool until you can handle them. Peel off the skins. Cut in half and remove any pits or cores using a melon baller. Spoon the fruit into dessert glasses, bowls, or wineglasses. Serve with your choice of garnish.

NOTES

▶ I prefer the oval-shaped Italian plums, but any variety of plum will be delicious here.

▶ First grate the zest with a Microplane, then cut the lemon in half and squeeze the juice.

MAPLE-PECAN BREAD PUDDING

DAIRY

MAKES 6 SERVINGS

This dish is my favorite winter Sunday morning breakfast. I assemble the pudding the night before, and wake up to a deliciously sweet treat.

The bread pudding can be stored in a covered container in the refrigerator for up to 3 days. To reheat gently, preheat the oven to 300°F. Place the pudding in a casserole and cover. Reheat in the oven for 15 to 20 minutes. The sauce can be stored, covered, in the refrigerator for up to 3 days. Reheat in a small saucepan over low heat.

FOR THE BREAD PUDDING

- 2 tablespoons (¼ stick) unsalted butter, melted, plus extra for greasing the insert
- One 1- to 1½-pound challah, sliced 1½ inches thick
- 4 large eggs
- 2 cups half-and-half
- 2 cups whole milk
- 1 cup tightly packed light brown sugar
- ½ cup granulated sugar
- ¼ cup best-quality maple syrup
- 2 teaspoons vanilla extract
- ½ cup chopped toasted pecans (see page 199)

- 1 tablespoon ground cinnamon
- ½ teaspoon freshly grated nutmeg

FOR THE MAPLE-PECAN SAUCE

- 1½ cups best-quality maple syrup
- ½ cup honey, preferably raw honey
- 1 tablespoon ground cinnamon
- ½ cup chopped toasted pecans (see page 199)

1. **Make the Bread Pudding.** Generously butter a 6½-quart slow cooker insert.
2. Arrange the challah slices in the insert in layers.
3. In a large bowl, whisk together the eggs, half-and-half, milk, sugars, maple syrup, vanilla, pecans, cinnamon, and nutmeg. Pour the custard over the bread. Cover and cook on High for 3 hours.
4. **Make the Maple-Pecan Sauce.** Combine the maple syrup, honey, cinnamon, and pecans in a small saucepan and bring to a boil. Turn down the heat and simmer for 10 minutes.
5. Scoop the warm bread pudding into bowls or dessert glasses. Serve the sauce warm, poured over the bread pudding.

OATMEAL WITH ALL THE "FIXINS"

MAKES 4 TO 5 SERVINGS

If you have never tried steel-cut oats, you are missing out on a breakfast treat. These chewy, nutty-flavored nuggets are power packed with nutrition. Quick-cooking oats have all of the nutrition, flavor, and texture processed out of them. Slow-cooked oats retain their al dente texture.

I like to add dried fruit, cinnamon, and a pat of butter to my bowl, while my kids like honey and chocolate chips. When they are fearlessly facing a bowl of healthy stick-to-your-ribs oats, I let the extra dose of chocolate slide. This oatmeal is pareve unless you opt for butter or heavy cream as a garnish, which will make it dairy.

The oatmeal is best served immediately after cooking but in a pinch can be stored, covered, in the refrigerator for 2 days. To reheat the oatmeal, add several tablespoons of water and gently reheat in a saucepan on the stovetop.

2 cups steel-cut oats

4 cups water

¼ cup tightly packed light brown sugar

1 tablespoon ground cinnamon

¼ teaspoon freshly grated nutmeg

SUGGESTED GARNISHES
Butter, ground cinnamon, dried fruit, fresh fruit, heavy cream, chocolate chips, honey

1. Place the oats, water, brown sugar, cinnamon, and nutmeg in a slow cooker insert. Stir to combine. Cover and cook on Low for 8 hours.

2. Ladle the oatmeal into bowls. Serve with or stir in the toppings of your choice.

Sauces

One of the very nicest things about life is the way we must regularly stop
whatever it is we are doing and devote our attention to eating.
—LUCIANO PAVAROTTI

Sauce making is one of my favorite tasks in the kitchen. For me, a sauce is not optional—it is integral to a dish. No matter how tired or uninspired I am, I still manage to come up with what I consider to be the oh-so-important icing on the cake. I like to think of sauce as a communication, a love letter perhaps. I speak to my family, my friends, and my customers through my food, especially sauces. I get to put my own personality into the food. A rich liquid full of flavor and soul is me speaking, not a company or corporation. I never get my sauces out of a jar or can. Those products are salty, lacking in freshness, and uninspired. Homemade sauces are made with fresh ingredients and wholesome products. When you are in the driver's seat, you are in control of what your family eats.

The flavors in a sauce should balance each other: The sauce should not be too sweet or too sour—just right. Sauce should also complement the food it is meant to garnish. Big beef flavor requires an assertive sauce; delicate fish needs something else entirely.

Like everything else, good sauce making can be time consuming. That is where the slow cooker comes in. A quick assembly of ingredients from a well-stocked pantry and you are in business. The slow cooker gently coaxes flavors and aromas out of ingredients. Before I ever thought of using my slow cooker for sauce making, I used to load a Dutch oven and put it in the oven. What I realized is that I was mimicking a slow cooker.

PARSLEY SAUCE

PAREVE MAKES $^1\!/_2$ CUP

This is my version of the classic accompaniment for Boiled Beef with Vegetables (page 66). The fresh flavors liven up the meat and vegetables, and the bright green color makes a beautiful presentation. Serve this versatile sauce separately or drizzle it generously over the dish. I keep parsley sauce on hand often and use it to perk up chicken, beef, and fish.

The sauce can be stored, covered, in the refrigerator for up to 2 days. If you place plastic wrap or parchment paper directly on the surface of the sauce, it can keep for up to 5 days.

¼ cup extra-virgin olive oil
2 cups fresh flat-leaf parsley leaves
2 tablespoons capers, drained and rinsed
1 garlic clove, coarsely chopped
Kosher salt and freshly ground black
    pepper

Place the olive oil, parsley, capers, and garlic in a blender or food processor. Process until the mixture resembles a loose paste. Season with salt and pepper. Serve or store.

HARISSA

MAKES $^1/_2$ CUP

This is an essential ingredient in Moroccan cooking. It is also my son Jonah's favorite hot sauce. It is fiery hot, but also has flavor and depth. I use it in the professional kitchens when food needs a "kick." I use harissa to give eggs and egg salad some excitement. In a pinch I toss couscous with it and add it to soups for a little extra zing. Jonah uses it on absolutely everything.

Harissa will keep for months, covered, in the refrigerator.

1 cup water

½ cup chili flakes

1 cup extra-virgin olive oil

1 garlic clove, coarsely chopped

¼ teaspoon ground cumin

1 tablespoon fresh lemon juice

2 tablespoons charnushka (see Note, page 109)

Kosher salt and freshly ground black pepper

PAREVE

1. Place a small saucepan over high heat and bring the water to a boil.
2. Remove the pan from the heat and stir in the chili flakes. Let the chili flakes steep for 5 minutes to rehydrate them.
3. Drain the flakes in a fine-mesh strainer.
4. Place the chili flakes, olive oil, garlic, cumin, lemon juice, and charnushka in a blender. Process until the mixture is a smooth paste. Season with salt and pepper. Serve or store.

NOTE

▶ Charnushka, a slightly smoky, pungent spice, is also called black caraway, nigella, and kalonji. It is not, however, the same thing as black cumin. Charnushka is commonly found in Middle Eastern cuisines as well as Indian spice mixes such as garam masala. (See Sources, page 233.)

BRAISED CIPOLLINI ONIONS IN MUSHROOM-PEPPERCORN SAUCE

MEAT

MAKES ABOUT 5 CUPS

This delicious sauce is perfect over slow-cooked pieces of meat as well as quickly grilled or pan-roasted steaks or chicken. The secret is the slow extraction of flavors from the cipollini, peppercorns, and mushrooms. This slightly sweet sauce is perfect over Meatloaf (page 96) and Rubbed Brisket (page 64). It is also perfect tossed with pasta or your favorite grain.

Cipollini are a slightly sweet onion that is actually the root of the grape hyacinth plant. They can be found in the early fall in many supermarkets as well as farmers' markets. They are a good pantry onion as they will maintain their flavor for several months.

The onions and mushrooms will keep in the sauce in a covered container in the refrigerator for up to 3 days. Reheat gently in a saucepan over low heat. I don't recommend freezing, as the onions and mushrooms will soften.

1 teaspoon whole black peppercorns

1 teaspoon whole white peppercorns

2 teaspoons dried whole green peppercorns

2 teaspoons whole pink peppercorns

Olive oil

2 pounds peeled cipollini onions (see page 115)

3 ounces cremini mushrooms with their stems, cut in half (about 1 cup)

3 garlic cloves, thinly sliced

¼ cup tomato paste

¼ cup balsamic vinegar

1 ounce (¼ cup) dried porcini mushrooms

½ cup brandy

2 cups dry red wine such as cabernet sauvignon

2 cups Essential Chicken Stock (page 207)

6 thyme sprigs

1 bay leaf

1. Preheat a slow cooker to High.

2. Toast the peppercorns in a small dry sauté pan over medium-high heat until they have darkened and are slightly smoky and very fragrant, about 7 minutes. (This helps mellow the peppercorns and gives them a deeper, smoky flavor. I recommend opening a window for this process as it can be smoky.)

3. Place a large sauté pan over medium heat. Lightly coat the bottom of the pan with olive oil. Cook the cipollini onions until they are browned, 3 to 5 minutes. Transfer the onions to the slow cooker insert.

4. Add the cremini mushrooms to the sauté pan. Add more oil, if necessary. Brown the cremini mushrooms about 5 minutes. Add the garlic toward the end of cooking the mushrooms and cook for 3 minutes more, until the garlic is slightly softened and very fragrant. Transfer the mushrooms to the slow cooker insert.

5. Add a little more olive oil to the sauté pan. Add the tomato paste and brown it, stirring constantly. This will take only about 3 minutes. Add the balsamic vinegar and simmer the mixture until the balsamic is reduced to a glaze. Transfer the mixture to the insert.

6. Add the porcini mushrooms, brandy, wine, stock, thyme, and bay leaf to the insert. Cover and cook on High for 4 hours.

7. Remove the thyme stems and bay leaf before serving or storing.

ROOT BEER BBQ SAUCE

PAREVE

MAKES 3 CUPS

I will often go out of my way for a mug of cold, bubbly root beer. So why not a BBQ sauce that sings with the earthy spice that I love? This is my version of the regional American sauce. I use it on chicken, short ribs, and brisket.

You can store this sauce, covered, in the refrigerator for up to 1 week, or freeze it for up to 3 months.

2 cups root beer such as Virgil's
   (don't use diet root beer)
1 cup ketchup, preferably Heinz
¼ cup fresh lemon juice
¼ cup fresh orange juice
¼ cup bourbon or apple cider for a nonal-
   coholic sauce
½ cup crumbled gingersnaps (about 8
   small cookies; store-bought are fine)

1½ tablespoons dark brown sugar
1 tablespoon light molasses
½ teaspoon minced lemon zest
½ teaspoon cayenne pepper (optional)
½ teaspoon ground ginger
2 garlic cloves, grated with a Microplane
1 medium onion, grated with a
   Microplane or on the fine side of a
   box grater
2 teaspoons kosher salt
1 tablespoon freshly ground black
   pepper

Place all of the ingredients in a slow cooker insert. Cover and cook on High for 6 hours. Adjust the salt and pepper to taste. Serve or store.

HOMEMADE AÏOLI

PAREVE

MAKES ABOUT 1 CUP

Aïoli is a wonderful, creamy condiment. I use it for garnishing Boiled Beef with Vegetables (page 66), where the tart, garlicky flavor accents the beefy flavor of the meats. I like to toss my coleslaw (page 149) with aïoli instead of mayo and pile the slaw on top of Rubbed Brisket (page 64) and slather the whole thing in Root Beer BBQ Sauce (page 184).

Homemade aïoli is fresh and tastes bright. It is in a class by itself and a completely different condiment than a jarred product. I like to keep a batch of it on hand for sandwiches, garnishes, and salad dressings.

Aïoli can be stored in the refrigerator, covered, for up to 3 days.

2 garlic cloves, grated with a Microplane

1 egg yolk

1 teaspoon Dijon mustard

1 tablespoon water

1 tablespoon fresh lemon juice

¾ cup neutral-flavored oil such as canola (you may not need all the oil)

Kosher salt and freshly ground black pepper

1. Place the garlic, egg yolk, Dijon mustard, water, and lemon juice in a large nonreactive bowl. Whisk together until smooth. Slowly drizzle in the oil while continually whisking. The mixture should resemble a loose mayonnaise. Add salt and pepper to taste.

2. You can also make this delicious aïoli in the food processor. Lightly pulse the garlic, egg yolk, mustard, water, and lemon juice until combined. With the motor running, drizzle the oil in a steady stream until the mixture becomes thick and creamy. Add salt and pepper to taste. Serve or store.

VARIATION

For Horseradish Aïoli, whisk 1 tablespoon prepared white horseradish into the aïoli. If you are using this recipe for Passover, use 1 cup store-bought kosher mayonnaise or leave out the mustard and substitute Passover-approved oil for the canola oil.

HERBED AÏOLI DIPPING SAUCE

PAREVE

M A K E S   A B O U T   1 $^1/_2$ C U P S

This dipping sauce is the perfect foil for Hot Wings (page 23). The cool creaminess readies your palate for another bite of spice. It also makes a great dressing for Creamy Coleslaw (page 149). Store in the refrigerator, covered, for up to 3 days.

**1 cup Homemade Aïoli (page 185) or
   store-bought mayonnaise**
¼ cup chopped fresh flat-leaf parsley
2 tablespoons chopped fresh chives
2 tablespoons chopped fresh tarragon
1 tablespoon fresh lemon juice
1 small shallot, grated with a Microplane
1 garlic clove, grated with a Microplane

Whisk together the aïoli, parsley, chives, tarragon, lemon juice, shallot, and garlic in a medium bowl. Serve or store.

CHARMOULA

PAREVE

MAKES ABOUT 1 CUP

This can be used as a condiment or marinade. The citrusy-herby flavors are just the right note for Chick Pea and Lentil Soup (page 35). I also recommend you add it as a garnish when you serve Lamb Tagine (page 104). The vivid flavors and color perfectly accent the earth spices of the tagine. It has a bright zippy flavor that brings out the earthiness of Middle Eastern spices—you might call it the Middle Eastern answer to the Italian Gremolata (page 191).

You can store charmoula, covered, in the refrigerator for up to 3 days. If the olive oil becomes solid, allow the charmoula to sit at room temperature for 1 hour.

**2 teaspoons cumin seeds, toasted
(see page 199)**

1 teaspoon chili flakes

1 garlic clove, grated with a Microplane

Juice of 1 lemon

Juice of 1 lime

**½ cup loosely packed fresh flat-leaf
parsley leaves**

½ cup loosely packed fresh cilantro leaves

⅓ cup extra-virgin olive oil

**Kosher salt and freshly ground black
pepper**

Place the cumin, chili flakes, garlic, lemon and lime juices, parsley, cilantro, and olive oil in a food processor. Process until a paste is formed. Season to taste with salt and pepper. Serve or store.

VARIATION

To make charmoula a more "traditional" way, combine the cumin, chili flakes, garlic, lemon and lime juices, parsley, and cilantro in a mortar. Pound with the pestle until it becomes a chunky paste. Drizzle in the olive oil a little at a time and continue pounding, until the mixture is completely chopped and a paste is formed. Season with salt and pepper.

TOMATO CHUTNEY

PAREVE

MAKES 2 ½ CUPS

I like to use heirloom tomatoes for this brightly colored and flavored chutney, which I dollop onto steaks, chicken, and fish. The tangy flavors of the chutney dress up every dish. I also serve it like a salsa, with chips and vegetable crudité.

The chutney can be stored, covered, in the refrigerator for up to 1 week, or frozen for up to 3 months.

5 pounds ripe tomatoes

8 whole peeled garlic cloves

3 shallots, peeled and thinly sliced

3 tablespoons extra-virgin olive oil

½ teaspoon chili flakes

1 teaspoon coriander seeds, toasted (see page 199) and cracked (see Note)

½ teaspoon fennel seeds, toasted (see page 199) and lightly crushed (see Note)

1 teaspoon mustard seeds

2 teaspoons charnushka (see Note, page 109)

1 teaspoon grated peeled fresh ginger

6 thyme sprigs, tied together with kitchen twine

½ cup golden raisins

One 2- to 3-inch cinnamon stick

¼ cup apple cider vinegar

¼ cup chopped fresh cilantro

¼ cup chopped fresh flat-leaf parsley

2 teaspoons fresh lemon juice

Kosher salt and freshly ground black pepper

1. Prepare an ice-water bath. Bring a large saucepan of water to a simmer. Cut a shallow X in the bottom of each tomato. Place the tomatoes in the simmering water for 30 seconds. Remove the tomatoes with a wire skimmer and immediately drop them into the ice water. When they are cool, peel off and discard the skins.

2. Cut the tomatoes into quarters. Gently squeeze out and discard the seeds.

3. Line a large fine-mesh strainer with cheese-cloth and place it over a bowl. Chop the tomatoes into large pieces. Place them into the cheesecloth-lined strainer. Place a plate over the tomatoes and weight with several cans on top. Allow the tomatoes to drain for 3 hours, or overnight in the refrigerator.

4 Reserve the liquid drained from the tomatoes for use in vinaigrettes. This water or essence has a pure, fresh tomato flavor.

5 Place the drained tomatoes, garlic, shallots, olive oil, chili flakes, coriander, fennel, and mustard seeds, charnushka, ginger, thyme, raisins, cinnamon, and vinegar into a slow cooker insert. Cover and cook on low for 8 hours.

6 Transfer the chutney to a bowl. Remove the thyme stems. Stir in the cilantro, parsley, and lemon juice. Season to taste with salt and pepper. Serve or store.

NOTES

▶ Place the toasted seeds on a cutting board and use a kitchen towel to form a ring around them (this keeps the seeds from falling off the cutting board). Gently press down on the seeds with a kitchen mallet or the back of a pan to release the essential oils that flavor the food. This process also helps the seeds soften while cooking.

▶ Charnushka, a slightly smoky, pungent spice, is also called black caraway, nigella, and kalonji. It is not, however, the same thing as black cumin. Charnushka is commonly found in Middle Eastern cuisines as well as Indian spice mixes such as garam masala. (See Sources, page 233.)

SPICY TOMATO SAUCE

PAREVE

MAKES 8 CUPS

I like to make a large batch of this spicy sauce in the slow cooker and then freeze it in resealable plastic storage bags for easy access.

Olive oil

2 large Spanish onions, diced

10 garlic cloves, minced

2 tablespoons dried thyme

2 tablespoons dried rosemary

2 red bell peppers, roasted (see page 37), stemmed, seeded, peeled, and chopped

Two 28-ounce cans whole peeled plum tomatoes with their juices, crushed (see page 8)

Three 15-ounce cans or 1½ large 28- to 29-ounce cans tomato puree

One 6-ounce can tomato paste

About 3 tablespoons chili flakes (more or less to taste)

Kosher salt and freshly ground black pepper

½ cup chopped fresh flat-leaf parsley

½ cup torn or chopped fresh basil leaves

1. Preheat a 6½-quart slow cooker to High. Place a large sauté pan over medium heat. Lightly coat the bottom of the pan with olive oil. Cook the onions until they are lightly browned and softened. Add the garlic and cook until the garlic has softened, about 5 minutes.

2. Transfer the onions to the slow cooker insert. Add the thyme, rosemary, roasted peppers, tomatoes with their juices, tomato puree, tomato paste, and chili flakes to the insert. Cook the sauce on High for 6 hours.

3. Adjust the seasoning with salt and pepper. Stir in the parsley and basil. If storing, let the sauce cool completely first.

GREMOLATA

PAREVE

MAKES ABOUT 1 CUP

Some people like their gremolata finely ground in a mortar and pestle. I prefer mine a bit chunkier, because I think the flavors tend to be brighter this way. Either way, it is delicious.

Gremolata can be made 1 day ahead of serving and stored, covered, in the refrigerator.

½ cup chopped fresh flat-leaf parsley

2 garlic cloves, finely minced

Finely grated zest and juice of 1 lemon (see Note)

Finely grated zest and juice of 1 orange (see Note)

3 tablespoons best-quality extra-virgin olive oil

Kosher salt and freshly ground black pepper

Combine the parsley, garlic, lemon and orange zests and juices, and olive oil in a small bowl. Stir to combine. Season to taste with salt and pepper. Serve or store.

NOTE

▶ First grate the zest with a Microplane, then cut the fruit in half and squeeze the juice.

SPARKLING SABAYON

PAREVE

MAKES 2 CUPS

I make this simple sauce when I want to dress up a quick pareve dessert. You can customize it to fit your taste and pantry ingredients. As in all pareve recipes, use the best ingredients possible. Use a good-quality sparkling wine and the best vanilla you can find. You don't have to spend a fortune on the wine; there are many great kosher sparkling wines and Champagnes on the market. Enjoy a glass or two while you're making this sauce and maybe this will become a regular recipe in your repertoire.

The sabayon can be stored in a tightly covered container in the refrigerator for 1 day.

½ cup sugar

Seeds scraped from ½ split vanilla bean

1 cup sparkling wine or Champagne
(leftover wine works well)

6 large egg yolks

½ teaspoon cornstarch

① Place a nonreactive metal bowl over a pan of simmering water. Do not allow the bowl to touch the surface of the water.

② Place the sugar, vanilla seeds, and sparkling wine in the bowl. Whisk the mixture until the sugar has completely dissolved. Add the egg yolks and cornstarch and whisk constantly until the mixture has tripled in volume and an instant-read thermometer reads 140°F (the temperature recommended for egg safety).

③ Remove the bowl from over the water and continue whisking for several minutes until the mixture has cooled. Serve or store.

RASPBERRY COULIS

PAREVE

MAKES 1 1/2 CUPS

A coulis is simply a thick, intensely flavored puree. A drizzle of a sumptuous coulis can brighten a simple brownie or slice of pound cake and turn it into a masterpiece. This particular version strays from the typical French-style sauce because it is not cooked. I love its vibrant color and sparkling flavor.

This coulis can be stored, covered, in the refrigerator for up to 1 week, or frozen for several months.

**3 cups fresh raspberries or thawed
    frozen raspberries
1 cup sugar
2 tablespoons fresh lemon juice**

Place the raspberries, sugar, and lemon juice in a blender. Process until the berries are completely broken up. Do not overprocess, as the seeds will be crushed. Strain the sauce through a fine-mesh strainer to remove the seeds. Adjust the sauce with additional sugar or lemon juice to taste. Serve or store.

Basic Recipes

Enjoying meals with my family is always the highlight of my day. I try to make even the simplest dishes taste as satisfying and delicious as possible. Learning to "work" each ingredient by adding aromatic spice and herb mixes and rich, full-bodied stocks, and using some simple kitchen techniques will make every meal, even the casual ones, delicious and memorable.

Every dish you make can be special just by using a few quality ingredients. I think of these recipes as fundamental building blocks. The spice mixes and stocks provide your foundation for great dishes and flavors.

Spice Mixes

I always make my own spice mixes. I like the idea that I can customize every dish with a spice mix, and I enjoy combining flavors and aromas to create my mixes. Sometimes I can take an existing mix, alter it slightly, and have an entirely new dish. These mixes are what keep food from becoming boring. Sure, you can cook a great piece of meat with vegetables, plain, and have a nice meal. Or you can add a little pizzazz with a spice mix or rub and wow your family and friends. Spice mixes are a perfect companion to a slow cooker. The long cooking time allows the flavors and aromas to mingle with meats, grains, and stocks to create luscious, aromatic dishes.

When I create a spice mix, I use the highest-quality spices and steer clear of artificial ingredients. I also make small batches of my mixes, store my spices in jars with tight-fitting lids, and keep them away from sunlight—that way the spices don't dry out and lose their potency.

HERBES DE PROVENCE

PAREVE

MAKES ABOUT $^1/_2$ CUP

I use this herb mixture so often that its container has come to feel like an extension of my arm. Herbes de Provence bring out the best in chicken, meats, fish, and vegetables. It is delicious in braised dishes and with caramelized onions. I think this fragrant mix is essential in Veal Ragout (page 102) and Osso Buco (page 99).

3 tablespoons dried marjoram
3 tablespoons dried thyme
1 tablespoon dried summer savory
1 tablespoon dried lavender
1 tablespoon dried basil
½ teaspoon crushed dried rosemary
½ teaspoon dried crumbled sage
½ teaspoon fennel seeds

Mix together all the ingredients in a small bowl. Store in a tightly covered container away from light for up to 3 months.

ALL-PURPOSE SPICE RUB

MAKES ABOUT $^1/_2$ CUP

I call this my all-purpose rub because it really does work for just about everything. I use it as a dry marinade on my Rubbed Brisket (page 64). I rub it on the meat and allow to sit for at least several hours or overnight. Then I proceed with the recipe. The rub is also delicious on chicken and fish.

1 tablespoon dry mustard
2 tablespoons Ancho Chile Powder
    (page 200, or see Sources, page 233)
1 teaspoon cayenne pepper
2 teaspoons light brown sugar
1 tablespoon finely grated orange zest
1 tablespoon pimenton (see Note,
    page 65)
2 teaspoons garlic powder

2 teaspoons onion powder
1 teaspoon kosher salt
1 teaspoon freshly ground black pepper

Whisk together all the ingredients. Because of the fresh orange zest, this spice mix should be stored in the refrigerator, in a tightly covered container. It will keep for up to 2 weeks.

NOTE

▶ Pimenton is a Spanish smoked paprika. It is really not comparable to the paprika found in most grocery stores. It may be sweet or hot, and has a wonderful smokiness essential to paella, chorizo, and other Spanish delicacies. Pimenton can be found readily online or at specialty markets. (See Sources, page 233.)

PAREVE

CURRY POWDER

MAKES ABOUT ³/₄ CUP

Curry powder, which is used in many Asian cuisines as well as African and Indian dishes, is actually a complex blend of spices. There are many variations on curry powder, depending upon where each specific curry originated. I have used curry powder in recipes for years but really became an enthusiast when I started playing with my own mix. I especially love using curry where you might expect it, in slow cooker soups like Senegalese Peanut Soup (page 51), and unexpectedly in entrées such as Shepherd's Pie (page 95). The flavors in the curry powder have time to perfume the ingredients and enhance the flavors of the components of the dish. Some Indian families keep their own blends guarded as family secrets. Why not formulate some family blends of your own?

3 tablespoons coriander seeds

1½ tablespoons cumin seeds

One 2- to 3-inch cinnamon stick, broken into pieces

2 tablespoons ground turmeric

1½ tablespoons cardamom seeds

½ teaspoon fenugreek seeds (see Note)

½ teaspoon cayenne pepper

2 tablespoons ground ginger

Combine the coriander, cumin, cinnamon, turmeric, cardamom, fenugreek, cayenne, and ginger in a spice grinder or coffee grinder. Process to a powder. Store in a tightly covered container away from light for up to 3 months.

NOTE

▶ Fenugreek is an ancient seasoning that has been found in excavation sites in the Middle East dating back to the Bronze Age. Sephardic Jews frequently eat fenugreek on Rosh Hashanah, as the Hebrew name for fenugreek means the same as "to increase merits." Both the leaves and seeds are commonly used in Middle Eastern and Indian recipes. (See Sources, page 233.)

TOASTING SPICES, SEEDS, AND NUTS

Toasting spices, seeds, and nuts heats up their natural oils, resulting in a very deep flavor and aroma.

Spices

Place spices in a small dry sauté pan over medium heat. Stir the spices occasionally until they have darkened slightly and are very fragrant, 2 to 5 minutes. Watch the spices carefully, as they can go from a perfect slightly darkened hue with a warm inviting fragrance to black and acrid in minutes. Transfer to a plate to cool before using.

Seeds

Place sesame seeds in a small dry sauté pan over medium heat. Stir occasionally until they have darkened slightly, about 1 minute. Transfer to a plate to cool before using.

Nuts

Place pine nuts in a small dry sauté pan over low heat. Stir occasionally until they are lightly browned. Watch them carefully, as they can go from perfect golden brown to unpalatable black in just a few moments. Cool before using.

Pecans and almonds may be toasted on the stovetop or in the oven. Hazelnuts and walnuts are best toasted in the oven. To toast nuts on the stovetop, place them in a small sauté pan over medium heat. Stir the nuts occasionally and cook until they are lightly browned and fragrant, about 5 minutes. Cool before using.

To toast nuts in the oven, spread them on a baking sheet and toast in a preheated oven at 350°F, stirring occasionally, until lightly browned and fragrant. (The time will vary for different nuts.) Cool before using.

ANCHO CHILE POWDER

PAREVE

MAKES ABOUT 1 TABLESPOON
POWDER FROM 1 MEDIUM
DRIED ANCHO PEPPER

Ancho chiles are dried poblano peppers. They have an earthy flavor and are mild to moderately hot. You can purchase dried ancho chiles from many grocery stores and Mexican markets or online (see Sources, page 233) and make your own powder. Look for soft, flexible chiles.

Ancho chiles, stemmed and seeded

Tear the chiles into pieces, place in a spice grinder or coffee grinder, and process to a powder. Strain out any large pieces and reprocess them. Store in a tightly covered container away from light for up to 3 months.

MOROCCAN SPICE MIX

MAKES ¼ CUP

PAREVE

This mix is a tour de force of flavor and fragrance. The complex aromas permeate meats, vegetables, and grains to give food a dynamic oomph. These flavors have a chance to do their magic in the slow cooker where they can spend many hours happily bubbling away. I use this mix often when I make Lamb Tagine (page 104) and Moroccan-Spiced Duck with Sweet-Tart Orange Sauce (page 120).

Two 2-inch cinnamon sticks, broken into pieces

1 tablespoon coriander seeds

1 teaspoon cumin seeds

1 teaspoon chili flakes

½ teaspoon fenugreek seeds (see Note, page 198)

½ teaspoon anise seeds

Seeds from 1 cardamom pod

1 teaspoon dark brown sugar (optional)

Place the cinnamon, coriander, cumin, chili flakes, fenugreek, anise, and cardamom seeds in a spice grinder and process until completely ground. If using the brown sugar, transfer the mixture to a small bowl and stir in the sugar. Store in a tightly covered container away from light for up to 3 months.

NOTE
▶ Fenugreek is an ancient seasoning that has been found in excavation sites in the Middle East dating back to the Bronze Age. Sephardic Jews frequently eat fenugreek on Rosh Hashanah, as the Hebrew name for fenugreek means the same as "to increase merits," a common theme during the High Holidays. Both the leaves and seeds are commonly used in Middle Eastern and Indian recipes. (See Sources, page 233.)

PORCINI DUST

PAREVE

MAKES ABOUT 3 TABLESPOONS
DUST FROM 1 OUNCE DRIED
PORCINI MUSHROOMS

This highly flavorful seasoning can be sprinkled on meat and vegetables during cooking.

1 ounce (¼ cup) dried porcini mushrooms

Process the mushrooms to a powder in a blender or food processor. Sift out any large pieces and reprocess them. Sift the final powder through a fine-mesh strainer. Store in a tightly covered container away from light for up to 3 months.

ZA'ATAR

MAKES ABOUT ³/₄ CUP

The slightly astringent quality of sumac, combined with the earthy flavors of hyssop and thyme, make za'atar a perfect spice mix for a vegetable platter or potatoes. A typical way of using za'atar in the Middle East is to dip bread into olive oil and then into za'atar. I sprinkle it on everything from my scrambled eggs to fresh salads to focaccia. I like to add extra zip to Braised Eggs in Spicy Tomato Sauce (page 134) by sprinkling za'atar on top of the eggs and cheese.

**2 tablespoons sesame seeds, toasted
(see page 199)**

¼ cup dried sumac (see Notes)

¼ cup dried thyme

**2 tablespoons sifted dried hyssop (see
Notes), put through a fine-mesh
strainer to remove any sticks**

Combine the sesame seeds, sumac, thyme, and hyssop in a small bowl. Store in a tightly covered container away from light for up to several months.

NOTES

▶ Sumac is an herb found throughout North America, the Middle East, and Europe. It has a lemony brightness that enhances meats, poultry, fish, and vegetables. (See Sources, page 233.)

▶ Hyssop is an herb with a slightly minty, thyme-like fragrance and flavor. It is mentioned many times in biblical passages and is thought to have been used for its healing properties. I like it for the herbaceous quality it adds to recipes. (See Sources, page 233.)

THAI RED CURRY PASTE

PAREVE

MAKES 2 CUPS

If you have never tried Thai food, this is a great place to start. Thai cooks are known for their passionate use of fresh ingredients. Unlike many spice mixes that rely upon the use of dried herbs and spices—and this recipe is really just another form of a spice mix—this paste uses mostly fresh, ripe ingredients lending it a heady perfume. Thai food is also known for its balance of the five flavors in each dish or in a single meal. They are: hot or spicy, sour, sweet, salty, and umami (a savory-salt flavor).

When I am stuck at home, I whir this paste together and I am immediately transported to an exotic locale. The spiciness can be controlled by cutting down the amount of chiles used.

Don't be intimidated by the number of ingredients. They all get tossed together into the blender. This paste is best used within a day or so of making. It can be frozen for up to 1 month.

3 small shallots or 1 small red onion, diced

2 lemongrass stalks, chopped (see Notes)

1 or 2 small fresh red chiles, preferably Thai bird chiles

5 large garlic cloves, coarsely chopped

One 3-inch piece peeled galangal (see Notes) or fresh ginger, coarsely chopped

1 tablespoon dark brown sugar

6 oil-packed anchovy filets, drained and chopped

1 heaping tablespoon whole coriander seeds, crushed (see Notes, page 189)

2 kaffir lime leaves (see Notes) or grated zest of 2 limes

½ cup packed fresh cilantro leaves and stems

1 tablespoon Curry Powder (page 198)

¼ cup unsweetened coconut milk

Process all the ingredients in a blender until the mixture is a thick paste. Store in a closed container.

NOTES

▶ Lemongrass has a soft citrus scent and flavor. To chop lemongrass, peel away the dry outer leaves until the soft pinkish center is revealed. Cut away the hard bottom part of the stalk and chop the 3 inches of soft inner core. Lemongrass is now widely available in produce markets and grocery stores, and in Asian groceries.

▶ Galangal and kaffir lime leaves can be found in some produce markets and in Asian and Indian grocery stores.

▶ Place the coriander seeds on a cutting board and use a kitchen towel to form a ring around them (this keeps the seeds from falling off the cutting board). Gently press down on the seeds with a kitchen mallet or the back of pan to release the essential oils that flavor the food. This process also helps the seeds soften while cooking.

Stocks

I always make my stocks from scratch. I know that if I make a great stock using only the freshest and best ingredients, I am halfway home to a great soup, sauce, or braised dish. The slow cooker makes stock making a snap. Before I discovered that the slow cooker was a great kitchen tool for everything that used to require hours of stovetop and oven cooking, I had to clear my schedule and plan way ahead of time to make something as simple as home-made chicken soup. Now, I make stocks weekly in my slow cooker. I gather my ingredients, pile them into the cooker, and turn it on. I can go to work or play while the slow cooker does all the work. The slow cooker doesn't require my attention, it doesn't heat up the house, and my freezer is always loaded with my arsenal of building blocks.

I store my stocks in covered containers in my refrigerator and freezer. Stock can be stored in the refrigerator, covered, for up to three days or may be frozen for up to three months.

I never add salt to my stocks. Because you cannot taste the stock as it cooks it is hard to tell how much salt is appropriate. Additionally, if you use the stock for a sauce that will be reduced, or a soup that has a long cook time, the salt will become concentrated and you can end up with an overly salty sauce or soup.

ESSENTIAL CHICKEN STOCK

MAKES 2 ½ QUARTS

Having a good stock in your kitchen arsenal is essential for full-flavored sauces and soups. Feel free to add your own touches such as mushroom stems or additional herbs and spices. While canned stock will do in a pinch, homemade ranks head and shoulders above it in richness and flavor. I always have a container of chicken bones in my freezer. When I have enough bones, I'll start up a batch of this stock.

I cool stock in a sink filled with ice water (this does the job quickly), then store the stock overnight in the refrigerator. This makes it easier to remove the fat that rises to the top and hardens.

Store in the refrigerator, covered, for up to 3 days, or freeze for up to 3 months.

3 to 4 pounds chicken bones (wings, carcasses, and necks)

1 large Spanish onion, roughly chopped

2 medium carrots, peeled and roughly chopped

1 celery stalk, roughly chopped

1 thyme sprig

5 flat-leaf parsley sprigs

1 bay leaf

1 whole clove

6 whole black peppercorns (about ¼ teaspoon)

Approximately 3 quarts water

1. Preheat a 6½-quart slow cooker to High.
2. Place the bones in the slow cooker insert and add the onion, carrots, celery, thyme, parsley, bay leaf, clove, and peppercorns. Cover the bones and vegetables with water only to the top of the bones. (If you add too much water, the flavor will be diluted.) Cover and cook on High for 6 to 8 hours. You know your stock is done when it has a deep yellowish color and tastes very rich in poultry flavor.
3. Strain the stock into a clean container and discard the bones and vegetables. Cool the stock completely, and ladle off the fat from the top of the stock.
4. Portion the stock into storage containers.

DARK CHICKEN STOCK

MEAT

MAKES 2 $^1/_2$ QUARTS

This is an incredibly rich stock with full flavor and rich color. Roasting the bones adds a deep intense flavor that would be too strong for many soups but it is just right for assertive braising liquids such as Braciole (page 82). It's a bit more trouble to make than the Essential Chicken Stock (page 207) but the extra flavor will make up for it. It is great for wine sauces and dark-colored soups.

Store in the refrigerator, covered, for up to 3 days, or freeze for up to 3 months.

3 to 4 pounds chicken bones (wings, carcasses, and necks)

1 large Spanish onion, roughly chopped

2 medium carrots, peeled and roughly chopped

1 celery stalk, roughly chopped

1 thyme sprig

5 flat-leaf parsley sprigs

1 bay leaf

6 whole black peppercorns (about ¼ teaspoon)

Approximately 3 quarts water

1 Preheat a 6½-quart slow cooker to High. Preheat the oven to 450°F.

2 Place the chicken bones on an unlined sheet pan and roast until dark brown, 15 to 20 minutes. Remove the bones from the sheet pan and place in the slow cooker insert. Drain off the fat from the sheet pan.

3 Add the onion, carrots, and celery to the sheet pan and roast until lightly browned, about 10 minutes. Add the vegetables to the bones.

4 Place the sheet pan over a stovetop burner on medium heat and add about 3 tablespoons water to the pan. Scrape off the browned bits (*sucs*; see page 7) with a wooden or silicone spatula. Pour the *sucs* and the liquid (it is loaded with flavor) into the slow cooker insert.

5 Add the herbs to the insert. Cover with water just to the top of the bones. Cover and cook on High for 6 to 8 hours. You will know the stock is done when a spoonful of the stock is a dark, rich brown color and the flavor is similar to roasted chicken.

6 Strain the stock into a clean container and discard the bones and vegetables. Cool the stock completely, and ladle off the fat from the top of the stock.

7 Portion the stock into storage containers.

TURKEY STOCK

MAKES 2 ½ QUARTS

Rich *and* delicious *are the two words that best describe this stock. I recommend using it for my Mole Poblano (page 118).*

After you cook a turkey, save the carcass and neck in the freezer until you are ready to make this stock.

Store in the refrigerator, covered, for up to 3 days, or freeze for up to 3 months.

1 carcass from a cooked turkey (about 3 pounds; see Note)

1 large Spanish onion, roughly chopped

2 medium carrots, peeled and roughly chopped

1 celery stalk, roughly chopped

1 thyme sprig

5 flat-leaf parsley sprigs

1 bay leaf

1 whole clove

6 whole black peppercorns (about ¼ teaspoon)

Approximately 3 quarts water

1. Preheat a 6½-quart slow cooker to High.
2. Place the turkey carcass in the slow cooker insert. Add the onion, carrots, celery, thyme, parsley, bay leaf, clove, and peppercorns. Cover the carcass and vegetables with water only to the height of the bones. (If you add too much water, the flavor will be diluted.) Cover and cook on High for 6 to 8 hours.
3. Strain the stock into a clean container and discard the bones and vegetables. Cool the stock completely, and ladle off the fat from the top of the stock.
4. Portion the stock into storage containers.

N O T E

▶ If the carcass does not fit easily into the insert, cut it through the breastbone.

VEAL STOCK

MEAT

MAKES 2 ½ QUARTS

Veal stock is like kitchen gold. It is an essential component in rich pan sauces and reductions. It can be hard to find a lot of veal bones, so create a standing order with your butcher to save bones for you. Store them in the freezer until you have a sufficient amount to make this stock.

Store the stock in the refrigerator, covered, for up to 3 days, or freeze for up to 3 months.

10 pounds veal shanks or knuckle bones

Olive oil

1 cup dry red wine such as cabernet sauvignon

3 large Spanish onions, coarsely chopped

1 leek, coarsely chopped (white part only)

3 medium carrots, peeled and coarsely chopped

2 celery stalks, coarsely chopped

2 medium tomatoes, cut in half

2 cups chopped mushroom stems

6 unpeeled garlic cloves

2 small bay leaves

10 flat-leaf parsley sprigs

5 thyme sprigs

6 whole black peppercorns (about ¼ teaspoon)

Approximately 3 quarts water, to just cover the bones

1. Preheat the oven to 450°F. Place the veal bones in a large roasting pan. Lightly rub the bones with olive oil and roast until browned but not scorched, about 1 hour.

2. Preheat a 6½-quart slow cooker to High. Transfer the bones to the insert of the slow cooker. Add the wine.

3. Add the onions, leek, carrots, celery, tomatoes, mushrooms, and garlic to the roasting pan and roast them, stirring occasionally, until browned and caramelized, 30 to 40 minutes. Add the vegetables to the bones. Scrape up any browned bits (*sucs*; see page 7) and juices, and add them to the insert.

4. Add the bay leaves, parsley, thyme, and peppercorns. Cover the ingredients with water just to their top. (Too much water will result in a weak and flavorless stock.) Cover and cook on High for 12 hours.

5. Strain the stock into a clean container and discard the bones and vegetables. Cool the stock completely, and ladle off the fat from the top of the stock.

6. Portion the stock into storage containers.

VEGETABLE STOCK

MAKES 2 ½ QUARTS

I always have lots of this versatile stock in my freezer. A kosher home really needs options for pareve dishes as well as meat meals. I use this stock for my soups, sauces, and grains and pastas such as couscous. Why use water when you can add something with good flavor?

Store the stock in the refrigerator, covered, for up to 1 week, or freeze for up to 3 months.

8 ounces cremini mushrooms with their stems, wiped clean and coarsely chopped

1 large Spanish onion, coarsely chopped

4 garlic cloves, coarsely chopped

Olive oil

1 medium red bell pepper, stemmed, seeded, and coarsely chopped

One 28-ounce can whole peeled plum tomatoes with their juices, crushed (see page 8)

1 large flat-leaf parsley sprig

1 large thyme sprig

1 medium fennel bulb, trimmed and coarsely chopped

1 celery stalk, coarsely chopped

2 medium carrots, peeled and coarsely chopped

6 whole black peppercorns (about ¼ teaspoon)

1 bay leaf

½ cup dry white wine such as chardonnay

Approximately 2 quarts water

1. Preheat a 5- to 6½-quart slow cooker to High. Preheat the oven to 400°F.
2. Place the mushrooms, onion, and garlic in a large bowl, and lightly toss with olive oil. Spread the vegetables on a sheet pan and roast in the oven until browned, about 15 minutes.
3. Place the roasted vegetables and the bell pepper, tomatoes, parsley, thyme, fennel, celery, carrots, peppercorns, bay leaf, and wine in the slow cooker insert. Cover with water only to the top of the vegetables. Cover and cook on High for 6 hours.
4. Strain the stock into a clean container and discard the vegetables. Cool the stock completely.
5. Portion the stock into storage containers.

BASIC RECIPES   ● 211

ROASTED GARLIC

PAREVE

MAKES 8 HEADS,
³/₄ CUP PUREE

The sweet, nutty flavor that results from roasting garlic is intoxicating. I use roasted garlic to "shmear" on chicken before I roast it, to thicken sauces, to add depth to pan sauces, and to add flavor to soups and stews.

Before my slow cooker addiction, I used to wrap the cut bulbs in foil and roast them in the oven, hoping that they would not be either too dark and acrid from overcooking or too hard to use from undercooking. Now I prep the garlic the same way and toss it in the slow cooker. I do a lot of garlic at a time, especially during the summer when the garlic is fresh and the cloves are very juicy. The slow cooker garlic is always soft and very sweet.

Store in the refrigerator for up to 2 weeks. The garlic can also be stored in the olive oil in the freezer for up to 2 months. To use, squeeze the soft garlic from the skins.

8 heads of garlic
¼ cup olive oil

1. Cut off the very top (the nonroot end) of the garlic heads. Discard the tops. Place the garlic on a large piece of aluminum foil. Drizzle with the olive oil.
2. Fold the foil into a large package, sealing the edges well. Place the package in the slow cooker. Cover and cook on Low for 8 hours.
3. Use immediately or transfer to a tightly covered jar or freezer container and cover the surface of the garlic with about ½ inch of olive oil. Cover and store.

PRESERVED LEMONS

MAKES 12 LEMONS
AND 4 CUPS OIL

I always have a jar of preserved lemons in the refrigerator at home and the cooler in my professional kitchen. The flavor and delicacy of texture cannot be found in any other ingredients or technique. I use these velvety lemons in Moroccan Chicken with Cracked Green Olives and Preserved Lemons (page 108) and Sweet Potato Salad with Preserved Lemons and Olives (page 145), and as a garnish for Lamb Tagine (page 104). This version of slowly cooking the lemons in olive oil is similar to poaching duck in duck fat. The gentle heat tenderizes the rind. The bonus is that you can use the oil for poaching fish or sautéing. It is full-flavored and delicious.

The lemons can be stored, covered, in the refrigerator for 1 month. Store the oil in a separate covered container and use to confit more lemons or poach fish (see Olive Oil–Poached Halibut, page 125), or for sautéing.

PAREVE

4 cups extra-virgin olive oil

12 lemons, washed and dried

3 whole peeled garlic cloves

6 whole black peppercorns
    (about ¼ teaspoon)

1 whole star anise

6 thyme sprigs

1 rosemary sprig

1 Place the olive oil, lemons, garlic, peppercorns, star anise, thyme, and rosemary in a slow cooker insert. Cover and cook on Low for 10 hours or until the lemons are very soft.

2 The lemons are ready to use immediately. Store the lemons and strained oil in separate containers.

MUSHROOM DUXELLES

PAREVE

MAKES 4 CUPS

To make duxelles, mushrooms are normally sautéed in a pan, requiring frequent stirring, but using the slow cooker makes it a snap. If you are a mushroom lover like me, this recipe is for you. I crave the deep, rich, earthy flavor. You can serve the mushrooms on toasted bread crisps, over polenta, with pasta, or use them as the flavor base for many recipes such as stews. The liquid also comes in handy.

You could use fancier mushrooms, but simple button mushrooms are delicious.

Store the mushrooms and liquid separately in the refrigerator for up to 5 days, or frozen for up to 2 months.

3 pounds button mushrooms, including stems, rinsed and thoroughly dried
3 large shallots, very finely chopped
2 garlic cloves, very finely chopped
½ cup dry white wine such as chardonnay
3 tablespoons olive oil
Kosher salt and freshly ground black pepper

1. Preheat a slow cooker to High. Pulse the mushrooms in a food processor in batches until they are finely ground but have not formed a paste.

2. Place the mushrooms, shallots, garlic, wine, and olive oil in the slow cooker insert and cook on High for 4 hours.

3. Season to taste with salt and pepper. Drain the mixture in a fine-mesh strainer over a bowl and reserve the liquid. Store the mushrooms and liquid in separate containers.

SOFRITO

MAKES ABOUT 4 CUPS

PAREVE

Sofrito is a Spanish word meaning "a well-cooked, aromatic sauce." Sofrito is typically used as a base to flavor other dishes including soups, sauces, and rice and bean dishes. Many cultures have a base similar to sofrito and there are many different recipes within each culture, with families claiming bragging rights as to who has the best recipe.

I think that sofrito adds a fresh, herbaceous flavor to many dishes. I like to make a big batch and then freeze it in small portions. I use it to give my soups, chilis, and other Latin dishes a zippy flavor.

Freeze for up to 6 months.

2 medium Spanish onions, cut into large chunks

3 cubanelle peppers, stemmed, seeded, and cut into chunks

3 heads of garlic, separated into cloves and peeled

3 medium tomatillos, husks removed, rinsed, and cut into chunks

1 bunch cilantro, including the attached stems and roots, well rinsed

3 large green bell peppers, stemmed, seeded, and cut into chunks

6 ripe plum tomatoes, cored and cut into chunks

1 large red bell pepper, stemmed, seeded, and cut into chunks

½ cup best-quality extra-virgin olive oil

1. Preheat a 6½-quart slow cooker to Low.
2. Process the onions, cubanelle peppers, garlic, tomatillos, cilantro, green bell peppers, tomatoes, and red pepper in batches in a food processor until they are chopped but not pureed. The texture should remain chunky.
3. Pour the olive oil into the slow cooker insert. Add the vegetables. Cover and cook on Low for 6 to 8 hours. The texture should resemble marmalade.
4. Portion the sofrito into small storage containers.

Recipes by Kosher Category

APPETIZERS

RECIPE / SUBRECIPE	PAREVE	MEAT	DAIRY
Hummos	●		
Cheese Fondue			●
Artichoke Caponata	●		
Mixed Olive Tapenade	●		
Sun-Dried Tomato Tapenade	●		
Chef Laura's Famous Guacamole	●		
Parmesan Crisps			●
Rosemary and Parmesan Popcorn			●
Hot Wings		●	
VIP Kreplach with Short Ribs		●	
Kreplach Dough	●		
Mushroom Terrine		●	
Peperonata with Crostini	●		
Tongue Salad with Horseradish Aïoli		●	

SOUPS

RECIPE / *SUBRECIPE*	PAREVE	MEAT	DAIRY
Chick Pea and Lentil Soup	●	●	
Primarily meat, but there is a pareve option.			
Tortilla Soup	●	●	●
Primarily pareve, but garnishes include dairy or meat, so could be any of the three.			
Black Bean Soup	●	●	●
Primarily pareve, but garnishes include dairy or meat, so could be any of the three.			
Creamy Tomato Soup			●
Vegetarian Chili	●		●
Primarily pareve, but garnishes include dairy.			
Ribollita	●		●
Primarily pareve, but there is a dairy option.			
Curried Split Pea Soup	●	●	●
Primarily pareve, but meat stock is an option and garnishes could include dairy.			
Onion Soup			●
Mulligatawny	●		●
Primarily pareve, but garnishes include dairy.			
Tomato and Basmati Rice Soup	●	●	
Primarily meat, but there is a pareve option.			
Pasta e Fagioli		●	
Sweet-and-Sour Cabbage Soup		●	
Senegalese Peanut Soup		●	
Italian Pumpkin Soup			●
Roasted Parsnip and Jerusalem Artichoke Soup			●
Wild Rice and Turkey Chowder		●	
Cauliflower-Apple Soup with Duck Confit			●
Bison Chili		●	

ENTRÉES

RECIPE / *SUBRECIPE*	PAREVE	MEAT	DAIRY
Rubbed Brisket		●	
Boiled Beef with Vegetables		●	
Garlicky Pot Roast		●	
Brown Sugar–Glazed Corned Beef		●	
Cholent		●	
Kishke	●	●	
Primarily meat, but there is a pareve option.			
Dafina		●	
Casserole of Beef and Peppers		●	
Braciole		●	
Sweet-and-Sour Belgian Beef and Onion Stew		●	
Cassoulet		●	
Falling-off-the-Bone Short Ribs		●	
Fava Bean and Lentil Stew	●		●
Primarily pareve, but garnishes include dairy.			
Stuffed Cabbage Rolls		●	
Tamales		●	
Tomatillo Sauce	●		
Shepherd's Pie		●	
Meatloaf		●	
Creamy Risotto with Italian Sausage, Peppers, and Onions		●	
Osso Buco with Gremolata and White Bean Ragù		●	
White Bean Ragù		●	
Veal Ragout		●	
Lamb Tagine		●	
Chicken with Rice		●	
Moroccan Chicken with Cracked Green Olives and Preserved Lemons		●	

ENTRÉES *continued*

RECIPE / *SUBRECIPE*	PAREVE	MEAT	DAIRY
Szechwan Chicken with Star Anise Sauce		●	
Spicy Chicken Meatballs		●	
Coq au Vin		●	
Curried Chicken		●	
Braised Turkey Breast in Mole Poblano		●	
Mole Poblano	●	●	
Primarily meat, but there is a pareve option.			
Moroccan-Spiced Duck with Sweet-Tart Orange Sauce and Forbidden Rice		●	
Forbidden Rice		●	
Duck Confit		●	
Sole with White Wine and Mushrooms		●	
Olive Oil–Poached Halibut	●		
Halibut Involtini	●		
Thai Fish Wrapped in Banana Leaves with Jasmine Rice	●		
Cucumber-Mint Relish	●		
Wild Mushroom Stroganoff			●
Smoky Navy Beans with Eggplant Ragù	●		
Braised Eggs in Spicy Tomato Sauce			●

SIDE DISHES

RECIPE / *SUBRECIPE*	PAREVE	MEAT	DAIRY
Brown Basmati Rice	●	●	
Primarily meat, but there is a pareve option.			
Couscous and Beans	●	●	
Primarily meat, but there is a pareve option.			
Cucumbers and Oranges in Rosewater	●		
Herbed Winter Squash	●	●	
Primarily meat, but there is a pareve option.			
Toasted Capellini (Angel Hair)	●	●	
Primarily meat, but there is a pareve option.			
Sweet Potato Salad with Preserved Lemons and Olives	●		
Simple Grits	●	●	
Primarily meat, but there is a pareve option.			
Cheesy Grits			●
Carrots with Dried Currants	●		
Creamy Coleslaw	●		
Lemon Risotto			●
Herbed Quinoa Pilaf	●	●	
Primarily meat, but there is a pareve option.			
Moroccan-Spiced Mixed Grain "Risotto"	●	●	
Primarily meat, but there is a pareve option.			
Kasha Varnishkes	●	●	
Primarily meat, but there is a pareve option.			
Mashed Sweet Potatoes	●	●	
Primarily meat, but there is a pareve option.			
Stewed Eggs	●		
Candied Kumquats	●		

DESSERTS AND BREAKFASTS

RECIPE / SUBRECIPE	PAREVE	MEAT	DAIRY
Black Forest Bread Pudding			●
Chocolate–Ancho Chile Pudding Cake with Sparkling Sabayon	●		
Wild Rice Pudding			●
Peach Melba	●		●
Primarily pareve, but garnishes include dairy.			
Flan			●
Key Lime Cheesecake			●
Persimmon Pudding	●		●
Primarily dairy, but there is a pareve option.			
Poached Pears with Sweet Mascarpone	●		●
Primarily dairy, but there is a pareve option.			
Poached Fruit Compote	●		●
Primarily pareve, but garnishes include dairy.			
Maple-Pecan Bread Pudding			●
Oatmeal with All the "Fixins"	●		●
Primarily pareve, but garnishes include dairy.			

SAUCES

RECIPE / SUBRECIPE	PAREVE	MEAT	DAIRY
Parsley Sauce	●		
Harissa	●		
Braised Cipollini Onions in Mushroom-Peppercorn Sauce			●
Root Beer BBQ Sauce	●		
Homemade Aïoli	●		
Horseradish Aïoli	●		
Herbed Aïoli Dipping Sauce	●		
Charmoula	●		

SAUCES *continued*

RECIPE / *SUBRECIPE*	PAREVE	MEAT	DAIRY
Tomato Chutney	●		
Spicy Tomato Sauce	●		
Gremolata	●		
Sparkling Sabayon	●		
Raspberry Coulis	●		

BASIC RECIPES

RECIPE / *SUBRECIPE*	PAREVE	MEAT	DAIRY
Herbes de Provence	●		
Curry Powder	●		
All-Purpose Spice Rub	●		
Ancho Chile Powder	●		
Moroccan Spice Mix	●		
Porcini Dust	●		
Za'atar	●		
Thai Red Curry Paste	●		
Essential Chicken Stock		●	
Dark Chicken Stock		●	
Turkey Stock		●	
Veal Stock		●	
Vegetable Stock	●		
Roasted Garlic	●		
Preserved Lemons	●		
Mushroom Duxelles	●		
Sofrito	●		

Holiday Menus

The slow cooker is an invaluable tool in my house *for making extraordinary dishes for the holidays.* The machine does all the hard work for me, properly browning ingredients and helping flavors mingle and blend together, while I focus on my other obligations. I can be the ultimate multitasker and turn out luxurious dishes with many courses and side dishes for my family and friends to feast on.

ROSH HASHANAH

When I dress my Rosh Hashanah table, I go for my best linens, fanciest dishes, and best serving pieces. I go all out for this holiday. And when I write my holiday menus, I also pull out all the stops.

This is my favorite time of year. The weather is beginning to change, fall is in the air, and there is a feeling of excited anticipation with the approaching holidays. It is also the craziest time of year for many families. Kids are going back to school, college kids are packed up and sent off, and everyone is adjusting to new schedules. I wish I had the time to just enjoy the season and let it unfold. Instead, the demands are heavy and time is short.

This is the time of year I like to pull out my slow cooker and put it to work around the clock. There seems to be this myth that slow cooker food is more casual and rustic. This is simply untrue. I have designed a menu for the high holiday that is elegant and sophisticated. The slow cooker will do much of the work and you can take all of the glory.

ROASTED PARSNIP AND JERUSALEM ARTICHOKE SOUP
page 54

This creamy, velvety soup is chic and sophisticated. I make the soup and freeze it before the holiday. The long cooking time for the parsnips is made simple with the slow cooker.

CAULIFLOWER-APPLE SOUP WITH DUCK CONFIT
page 56

This sounds complicated, but because the soup can be made several days ahead in the slow cooker, and the duck confit is also made ahead in the slow cooker and frozen, it really is doable. The soup makes use of autumn produce at its best, and is delicious by itself. You could easily serve the soup garnished with just some sautéed apples and a drizzle of honey. But the duck confit makes it a triumph. The slow cooker does all the work, and any extra confit can be frozen for the next batch of soup or for an elegant entrée.

VEAL RAGOUT
page 102

The luscious flavor of the sauce comes from the long cooking process, made easy in the slow cooker. This is the time of year to splurge on earthy porcini mushrooms and an elegant dry white wine for this dish. With fresh herbs as a garnish, this ragout will be a masterpiece that may become a new holiday tradition.

POACHED FRUIT COMPOTE
page 174

As summer is winding down, I like to take advantage of the farmers' market offerings. Stone fruits like peaches, plums, and end-of-season cherries are at their peak. Pear and apple varieties are appearing daily, each with a different color, flavor, and texture. What better way to wrap them all up in one delicious package than to poach them and let the flavors mingle and meld? The color of this compote is stunning and the bouquet is delicately scented with cinnamon. I like to add a vanilla bean and spoon the gorgeous fruit over chiffon cake or honey cake.

SUKKOT

Of all the holidays in the Jewish calendar, Sukkot is my favorite. Fall is in full swing and the cooler temperatures allow me to take advantage of rich flavors and heartier cuisine. The holiday celebrates the harvest and any dish that takes advantage of regional foods is a must-have on the menu. My slow cooker is often called into action to make short work of long-cooking vegetables and braised meats.

ITALIAN PUMPKIN SOUP
page 52

I like to whip up a large batch of this creamy soup and freeze it. The soup is rich and decadent—but it is also easy to make. The addition of porcini mushrooms, cabbage, and nutmeg give the soup its character. I like to serve it in a hollowed-out pumpkin that has been roasted for thirty minutes. The roasting gives the pumpkin a burnished look and a nutty flavor.

STUFFED CABBAGE ROLLS
page 90

This recipe is a must-have for at least one night during Sukkot. These miniature cornucopias symbolize a plentiful harvest. I make my stuffed cabbage a day or so ahead of serving. The flavors really develop and there is no last-minute rushing around.

BRACIOLE
page 82

The slow cooker takes tough cuts of meat and makes them fork-tender and delicious. Braciole is the perfect hearty dish to eat in the *sukkah*. Similar in idea to stuffed cabbage and other stuffed foods traditionally eaten during the holiday, Braciole requires a bit of assembly labor, but then does its thing in the slow cooker—including make its own sauce! Serve this mouthwatering dish with potatoes, rice, or couscous.

WILD MUSHROOM STROGANOFF
page 130

The great thing about Sukkot is that there are so many nights and so much food. I like to mix it up a bit with this hearty dairy recipe. I adore mushrooms, and this dish is all about big, rich, full-flavored mushrooms. The slow cooker allows the flavors to develop fully. Use your best wine, herbs, and mushrooms for this recipe.

POACHED PEARS WITH SWEET MASCARPONE
page 172

Quick and easy do-ahead poached pears are the perfect go-to dessert, and fall is the time to make them. Poach them gently in the slow cooker and store them in the refrigerator in their poaching liquid to enjoy this elegant dessert at your leisure.

HANNUKAH

This festival demands big, hearty flavors and textures to stand up to latkes, *sufganiyot* (jelly doughnuts), and other festive treats. I reach for rich and saucy meat dishes. Garlicky Pot Roast and Coq au Vin are perfect foils for crispy potato latkes.

Slow cooker ease means I don't fuss or fret over the main course. That way I have plenty of time and energy to make my latkes and doughnuts and keep everyone happy.

GARLICKY POT ROAST
page 68

I like to take a large platter and pile it high with latkes on one side. I take big, moist chunks of this rich roast and pile them next to the latkes. I spoon gravy over the meat and let the whole platter of goodness mingle. Roughly chopped parsley, thyme, and chives, sprinkled over, complete the dish.

COQ AU VIN
page 114

The complex flavors of wine, herbs, and mushrooms with a long slow-cooked flavor make this dish a family favorite and cold weather staple in my house. I used to roll my eyes when requests for the "drunken chicken" dish would mount up. All I could envision was me standing over a pot for hours while chicken, wine, and vegetables hung out together, gathering flavor.

Now I plan ahead. The day before I want to serve, I brown my chicken and vegetables and deglaze my pan. Then the next day I let the slow cooker make the dish for me. I can go to work, drive carpool, or whatever, and still have an elegant meal for my family.

PURIM

I always go for big-flavored dishes for this holiday. I suppose it is because the holiday originates in a part of the world where exotic spices perfume dishes and homes. I make my own spice mixes and want to give them the chance to work their magic on poultry, meats, and legumes. No quick sauté in a pan is going to do justice for the big flavors I am looking for. I need a long, slow cooking session to round out seasonings.

No problem—slow cooker to the rescue.

HUMMOS
page 14

I don't like canned chick peas. I cannot get past the canned flavor. I would rather spend a bit of time soaking them and loading them into the slow cooker and get a really great product than use the canned variety. Homemade hummos is a treat and everyone appreciates it. If you have leftovers, "shmear" it on bread, top with your favorite luncheon meats or roasted vegetables, and treat yourself to a healthy snack.

TOMATO AND BASMATI RICE SOUP
page 48

This soup can be made several days ahead of serving. I never get tired of it and make large batches to freeze.

LAMB TAGINE
page 104

Cooking lamb can be intimidating. But not when you use the slow cooker. This recipe merges exotic spices and assertive lamb flavors. Everyone loves this dish. The addition of dried fruits rounds out the aromatic vegetables. Lamb tagine is a crowd pleaser and can be made into a banquet with the addition of simple garnishes like chopped herbs, couscous, and preserved lemons.

PASSOVER

I used to characterize Passover (Pesach) as the "no rest for the weary" holiday. Between cleaning and cooking all of those meals and trying to spend some quality time with family, this holiday is no picnic! Then it dawned on me that investing in a slow cooker for the holiday might just save me time—and my sanity. It was well worth the expense. Now I can just prep the food and let the machine do the work while I hang out with my kids.

STEWED EGGS
page 156

These marbled eggs make a beautiful presentation, and their texture is creamy and velvety.

ARTICHOKE CAPONATA
page 16

Pesach is a transition holiday—not quite spring and not quite winter. I use this recipe as kind of a bridge between the seasons. My kids love artichokes. The larger variety are not in season yet, and the baby varieties are delicate and tastier anyway. I use this relish as a side dish for poultry, fish, or meats. We also eat it piled on matzah for snacks.

BROWN SUGAR–GLAZED CORNED BEEF
page 70

I love corned beef but don't want to sit around waiting for it. The slow cooker infuses it with flavor. I urge you to try this recipe. It will become a holiday tradition.

SOLE WITH WHITE WINE AND MUSHROOMS
page 123

We eat a lot of fish in our house. That may be due to our love of dairy desserts. I admit it—it is true. We also happen to really like fish. This is a delicate, elegant dish that looks fussy but isn't. My twist on the classic has all the flavors of the original but my version lets the cook rest on the couch—or wherever.

OLIVE OIL–POACHED HALIBUT
page 125

Poaching fish in olive oil in the slow cooker is brilliant. The slow cooker makes this technique fool-proof. The oil stays at an even temperature and never "fries" the fish. This flavorful method of cooking the first-of-the-season halibut is a treat. It is perfect for Pesach and while halibut remains in season.

SHAVUOT

This major festival is what my kids used to call "the cheesecake holiday." I suppose it is because of the "land of milk and honey" reference. It is also because if there is any chance to make cheesecake, I am inspired. I recently discovered that making cheesecake in the slow cooker is the way to go. Cheesecakes never crack. The slow, even temperature means a light and custardy cake as well. If you have an oval slow cooker, you can easily make cheesecake in a loaf pan or in ramekins.

THAI FISH WRAPPED IN BANANA LEAVES WITH JASMINE RICE
page 128

This full-flavored fish dish is a family favorite. It is also easier than the recipe looks. The sauce gets whirred together in the blender and can be made days ahead. The fish, wrapped in the banana leaves, cooks gently with the rice in the slow cooker. The whole assembly arrives at the table smelling exotic and tropical. The elegant presentation is unusual and very festive.

KEY LIME CHEESECAKE
page 168

Ari's favorite cheesecake is a holiday and year-round staple. The cheesecake is assembled and then cooked and cooled in the slow cooker. A quick chill in the refrigerator and dessert is served.

Sources

BEANS AND LENTILS

Beans and Lentils.com
www.beanslentils.com

Bulk Foods
www.bulkfoods.com

iGourmet.com
www.igourmet.com

CHOCOLATE AND COCOA POWDER

Chocosphere
www.chocosphere.com

FLOURS, CEREALS, AND DRIED FRUITS

Bob's Red Mill
www.bobsredmill.com

GRAINS AND RICES

Eden Organic
www.edenfoods.com

KOSHER BISON AND ORGANIC MEAT

Golden West Cattle Company
www.goldenwestglatt.com

NUTS, LEGUMES, AND SPICES

Nuts Online
www.nutsonline.com

POMEGRANATE MOLASSES AND PASTE

Sadaf
www.sadaf.com

SPICES, VANILLA BEANS, AND WHOLE CHILES

The Spice House
www.thespicehouse.com

Index